Workshop Manual

**BMW R 50/5
R 60/5
R 75/5**

Bayerische Motoren Werke AG München

Bestell-Nr. 01 51 9 099 051 e 1,0 IX. 69 Printed in Western Germany

INTRODUCTION

Welcome to the world of digital publishing ~ the book you now hold in your hand was printed using the latest state of the art digital technology. The advent of print-on-demand has forever changed the publishing process, never has information been so accessible and it is our hope that this book serves your informational needs for years to come. If this is your first exposure to digital publishing, we hope that you are pleased with the results. Many more titles of interest to the classic automobile and motorcycle enthusiast, collector and restorer are available via our website at www.VelocePress.com. We hope that you find this title as interesting as we do.

NOTE FROM THE PUBLISHER

The information presented is true and complete to the best of our knowledge. All recommendations are made without any guarantees on the part of the author or the publisher, who also disclaim all liability incurred with the use of this information.

TRADEMARKS

We recognize that some words, model names and designations, for example, mentioned herein are the property of the trademark holder. We use them for identification purposes only. This is not an official publication.

INFORMATION ON THE USE OF THIS PUBLICATION

This manual is an invaluable resource for those interested in performing their own maintenance. However, in today's information age we are constantly subject to changes in common practice, new technology, availability of improved materials and increased awareness of chemical toxicity. As such, it is advised that the user consult with an experienced professional prior to undertaking any procedure described herein. While every care has been taken to ensure correctness of information, it is obviously not possible to guarantee complete freedom from errors or omissions or to accept liability arising from such errors or omissions. Therefore, any individual that uses the information contained within, or elects to perform or participate in do-it-yourself repairs or modifications acknowledges that there is a risk factor involved and that the publisher or its associates cannot be held responsible for personal injury or property damage resulting from the use of the information or the outcome of such procedures.

WARNING!

One final word of advice, this publication is intended to be used as a reference guide, and when in doubt the reader should consult with a qualified technician.

INTRODUCTION

The purpose of this repair manual is to provide the necessary information to perform the required maintenance and repairs. It is most useful to a trained BMW specialist and supplements the knowledge he acquired during the training sessions in a BMW Service School.

Each main section is preceded by the corresponding specifications. The various groups are, according to the system, established in the flat rate manual.

Example:

    33–10/2 in the index means:
    33 Main section
    –10 Sub section
    / 2 Page number of the sub section.

The special tools that are available are listed in the Tool catalog, Part No. 01 99 9 099 420. The method with which these tools are used is illustrated in the appropiate section of this repair manual.

As a rule, the sequence of removal is explained. If the reassembly is not possible in reverse order of the removal, it is explained accordingly.

For any subsequent changes and additions, new sheets will be issued. They either replace existing sheets or they are added.

Additional information can be derived from Service Bulletins, and the illustrations in the parts catalog.

                                                                BAYERISCHE MOTOREN WERKE

11 Engine

Specifications		Page 3
11 00 050	Engine removal and installation	19
11 11 527	Cylinder boring and honing	22
11 12 100	Cylinder head removal and installation	23
11 12 503	Cylinder head disassembly, reassembly, and valve grinding	25
11 12 561	Valve guide replacement	27
11 12 621	Talve seat replacement	27
11 14 800	Timing cover removal and installation	28
11 21 501	Crankshaft replacement	30
11 21 531	Main bearing replacement	32
11 22 510	Flywheel removal and installation	36
11 24 500	Connecting rod removal and installation	37
11 24 551	Connecting rod bearing replacement	39
11 25 500	Piston removal and installation	40
11 31 061	Timing sprocket replacement	42
11 34 504	Adjusting Valve Clearance	45
11 41 500	Oil pump removal and installation	46

Specifications

Engine

	R 50/5	R 60/5	R 75/5
Type			
Engine type	Horizontally opposed with overhead valves		
Engine number location	On the left side of engine housing near the dip stick		
Bore mm	67 (2.68")	73,5 (3.07")	82 (3.2")
Stroke mm		70,6 (2.9")	
Number of cylinders		2	
Arrangement of cylinders	Horizontally-opposed		
Squareness ratio	1,05	0,96	0,86
Displacement ccm	498	599	745
Compression ratio	8,6 : 1	9,2 : 1	9,0 : 1
Horse Power HP at RPM	36/6600	46/6600	57/6400
Maximum permitted sustained RPM	6500	6500	6200
Maximum permitted RPM		7000	
Idle speed RPM		800÷1000	
Maximum permitted RPM during break-in			
to 600 Miles RPM		4000	
to 1200 Miles RPM		5000	
Direction of rotation	Clockwise (as viewed from the front)		
HP cu. inch	1.14	1.25	1.24
Maximum torque lb-ft at RPM	28.2 / 5000	35.5 / 5000	43.4 / 5000

Specifications

Engine

Type	R 50/5	R 60/5	R 75/5
Piston speed ft./sec. at RPM	49.5 / 6400	49.5 / 6400	48.0 / 6200
Compression lbs/inch² above average / average / poor		over 142.2 / 128÷142.2 / below 128	
Instructions for compression check		1- Remove spark plugs. 2- Using a calibrated compressometer, check compression wither battery fully charged, engine at normal operating temperature and wide open throttle. Turn engine over at starting speed, using electric starter for this check. Remove vacuum type carburetor prior to checking.	
Curb weight lbs.	129 (With carburator and oil, without ignition coils and intake system.)	139 "(with starter motor, carburetors and oil, without ignition coils and intake system)"	143
Recommended Fuel	Regular	Premium	Premium
Fuel consumption Miles/gallon	54.2	49	45.2

Specifications

Engine

Type	R 50/5	R 60/5	R 75/5
Engine lubrication system:			
		High pressure wet sump system	
Oil filter		Full flow	
Oil pump type		Rotary full pressure	
Oil pressure warning light lights at pressure atü lbs./square inch		0,2÷0,5	
Oil capacity without filter change Ltr. (quarts)		2 (2.11 US quarts / 1.76 Imp quarts)	
with filter change Ltr. (quarts)		2,25 (2.38 US quarts / 1.98 Imp quarts)	
Oil consumption (miles/quarts)		0,1 (0.106 US quarts / 0.088 Inmp quarts)	
Oil recommendation at ambient temperatures below 32° Fahrenheit		Brand name engine oil SAE 10W30	
between 32°–86° Fahrenheit		Single grade HD oil SAE 30	
over 86° F. and for high speed requirements		Single grade HD oil SAE 40	
Oil Pump:			
Pressure relieve valve opens at lbs./square inch		5,0 (71 psi)	
Oil pump output (qts/h) at RPM Ltr./h		1400 (1480 US quarts / 1230 Imp quarts) 6000	
Outer rotor clearance mm		0,1÷0,17 (0.004÷0.0068")	
Outer rotor diameter mm		$57{,}1 \begin{smallmatrix}0\\-0{,}025\end{smallmatrix}$ (2.21" $\begin{smallmatrix}0\\-0{,}001''\end{smallmatrix}$)	
Housing diameter mm		$57{,}2 \begin{smallmatrix}+0{,}046\\0\end{smallmatrix}$ (2.215" $\begin{smallmatrix}+0{,}00184''\\0\end{smallmatrix}$)	

8.69

Specifications

Engine	R 50/5	R 60/5	R 75/5
Type			
Rotor width mm		14 −0,016/−0,034 (0.551" −0.00064/−0.00136)	
Housing depth mm		14 +0,025/+0,010 (0.551" +0.001/+0.0004)	
Clearance between joint surface (pump body) and sealing surface (rotor) mm		0,050÷0,091 (0.002"÷0.004")	
Clearance between rotors mm		0,12÷0,30 (0.0048÷0.0012")	
Maximum allowable wear in cover mm		0,05 (0.002")	
Free length of relieve valve spring mm		68 (2.68")	
Valve Clearance:			
Adjusted with cold engine			
Intake valve		0,15 (0.006")	
Exhaust valve		0,20 (0.008")	
Valve timing		With valve clearance of 2 mm	
Intake opens	40° before TDC		10° before TDC ⎫
Intake closes	40° after BDC ⎫ ± 2,5°		50° after BDC ⎬ ± 2,5°
Exhaust opens	40° before BDC ⎬		50° before BDC ⎪
Exhaust closes	10° after TDC ⎭		10° after TDC ⎭
Valves:			
Length (overall) Intake mm	103,0−0,4 (4.05"−0.016")	98,5−0,3 (3.88"−0.012")	98,8−0,4 (3.89"−0.016")
Exhaust mm	102,5−0,4 (4.04"−0.016")	97,5−0,3 (3.84"−0.012")	98,8−0,4 (3.89"−0.016")
Head diameter Intake mm	34 (1.34")	38 (1.495")	42 (1.655")
Exhaust mm	32 (1.26")	34 (1.34")	38 (1.495")
Stem diameter intake	8 −0,040/−0,055 (0.315" −0.0016/−0.0022)	8 −0,050/−0,065 (0.315" −0.0020/−0.0026)	8 −0,050/−0,065 (0.315" −0.0020/−0.0026)

Engine

Specifications

Type	R 50/5	R 60/5	R 75/5
Exhaust valve shaft diameter mm	$8\,{-0,050 \atop -0,065}$ (0.315"${-0.0020 \atop -0.0026}$)	$8\,{-0,065 \atop -0,080}$ (0.315"${-0.0026 \atop -0.0032}$)	$8\,{-0,050 \atop -0,065}$ (0.315"${-0.0020 \atop -0.0065}$)
Minimum valve edge thickness Intake mm Exhaust mm		$1 \atop 1$ (0.04")	
Maximum valve head runout mm		0,025 (0.001")	
Valve Seat:			
Outer diameter Intake	$36,2\,{0 \atop -0,025}$ (1.425"${0 \atop -0.001}$)	$39,2\,{0 \atop -0,025}$ (1.544"${0 \atop -0.001}$)	$43,2\,{0 \atop -0,025}$ (1.7"${0 \atop -0.001}$)
Outer diameter Exhaust	$36,2\,{-0,050 \atop -0,060}$ (1.425"${-0.002 \atop -0.003}$)	$39,2\,{0 \atop -0,025}$ (1.544"${0 \atop -0.001}$)	$43,2\,{-0,050 \atop -0,066}$ (1.7"${-0.002 \atop -0.00264}$)
Bore diameter for valve Seat in cylinder head Intake mm	$36\,{+0,025 \atop 0}$ (1.418"${+0.001 \atop 0}$)	$39\,{+0,025 \atop 0}$ (1.535"${+0.001 \atop 0}$)	$43\,{+0,025 \atop 0}$ (1.694"${+0.001 \atop 0}$)
Exhaust mm	$36\,{+0,025 \atop 0}$ (1.418"${+0.001 \atop 0}$)	$39\,{+0,025 \atop 0}$ (1.535"${+0.001 \atop 0}$)	$43\,{+0,025 \atop 0}$ (1.694"${+0.001 \atop 0}$)
Shrink-fit in cyl. head Intake mm Exhaust mm To install new seats heat cyl. head to 464—500 degrees Fahrenheit	0,15÷0,20 (0.006"÷0.008") 0,10÷0,15 (0.004"÷0.006")	0,15÷0,20 (0.006"÷0.008") 0,15÷0,20 (0.006"÷0.008")	0,15÷0,20 (0.006"÷0.008") 0,10÷0,15 (0.004"÷0.006")
Valve seat angle		45°+20'	
Valve seat width:			
Intake mm		1,5 (0.06")	
Exhaust mm		2,0 (0.08")	

8.69

Specifications

Engine

Type	R 50/5	R 60/5	R 75/5
Valve seat oversizes mm		0,2 (0.008")	
Valve Guide:			
Full length mm		54 (2.13")	
Outer diameter mm		14 +0,061/+0,050 (0.551" +0.00244/+0.002)	
Inner diameter mm		8 +0,015/0 (0.315" +0.0006/0)	
Bore in cylinder head mm		14 +0,018/0 (0.551" +0.00072/0)	
Interference fit in cylinder head mm		0,032÷0,061 (0.00128÷0.00244)	
Cylinder head Fahrenheit		240÷260 (460÷500° F)	
Repair temperature mm			
Valve guide oversizes		14,1 +0,061/+0,050 (0.555" +0.00244/+0.002)	
Valve stem clearance:			
Intake mm	0,040÷0,070 (0.0016"÷0.0028")	0,050÷0,080 (0.002"÷0.0032")	0,050÷0,080 (0.002"÷0.0032")
Exhaust mm	0,050÷0,080 (0.002"÷0.0032")	0,065÷0,095 (0.0026"÷0.0038")	0,050÷0,080 (0.002"÷0.0032")
		0,15 (0.006")	
Valve actuation:			
Cam shaft/drive		Ohv through tappets push rods and rocker arms	
Cam chain		Duplex chain with chain tensioner	
		3/8 × 7/32	
Roller diameter mm		6,35 (0.25")	
Number of links		50	

Specifications

Engine

Type	R 50/5	R 60/5	R 75/5
Valve Springs:			
Wire diameter mm		4,25 (0.167")	
Outer diameter mm		31,9 (1.255")	
free length mm		ca. 43,5 (1.71")	
Spring load at length mm lbs./a" inches	29 Kp/37,6 mm (64 lbs./1.48")		70 Kp/28,5 mm (154.5 lbs./1.125")
Direction of winding		right	
Number of windings		6	
Installed position		Green painted winding toward cylinder head	
Rocker arm:			
Rocker arm bore diameter mm		18 +0,059/+0,032 (0.708" +0.00236/+0.00128)	
Outer diameter of rocker arm bushing mm		18 +0,030/+0,012 (0.708" +0.0012/+0.00048)	
Inner diameter of rocker arm bushing mm		14,5 +0,059/+0,032 (0.57" +0.00236/+0.00128)	
Rocker arm shaft diameter mm		14,5 +0,030/+0,012 (0.57" +0.0012/+0.00048)	
Clearance of rocker arm shaft mm		0,002÷0,047 (0.00008"÷0.00188")	
Rocker arm clearance mm		0,002÷0,047 (0.00008"÷0.00188")	
Rocker arm side play		No clearance (spring pre-load)	

Specifications

Engine

Type	R 50/5	R 60/5	R 75/5
Cam shaft			
Bore diameter for front cam shaft bearing flange mm		$40 \,{}^{+0,039}_{0}$ (1.575" ${}^{+0.00156}_{0}$)	
Diameter of front cam shaft bearing flange mm		$40 \,{}^{0}_{-0,016}$ (1.575" ${}^{0}_{-0.00064}$)	
Cam shaft, bearing flange inner diameter mm		$25 \,{}^{+0,021}_{0}$ (0.985" ${}^{+0.00084}_{0}$)	
Cam shaft, front bearing journal diameter ⌀ mm		$25 \,{}^{-0,020}_{-0,041}$ (0.985" ${}^{-0.0008}_{-0.00164}$)	
Cam shaft, rear bearing journal diameter ⌀ mm		$24 \,{}^{-0,020}_{-0,041}$ (0.945" ${}^{-0.0008}_{-0.00164}$)	
Bore diameter for rear cam shaft bearing ⌀ mm		$24 \,{}^{+0,021}_{0}$ (0.945" ${}^{+0.00084}_{0}$)	
Clearance mm		$0,020 \div 0,062$ (0.0008" ÷ 0.00248")	
End play mm		$0,1 \pm 0,02$ (0.004 ± 0.0008")	
Cam lift mm	6,198 (0.244")	6,198 (0.244")	6,756 (0.266")
Tappet diameter mm		$22 \,{}^{-0,025}_{-0,045}$ (0.866" ${}^{-0.001}_{-0.0018}$)	
Tappet bore in engine housing mm		$22 \,{}^{+0,006}_{-0,015}$ (0.866" ${}^{+0.00024}_{-0.0006}$)	
Tappet clearance in engine housing mm		$0,01 \div 0,051$ (0.0004" ÷ 0.00204)	

Specifications

Engine

Type	R 50/5	R 60/5	R 75/5
Crankshaft and Bearings:			
Main bearing journal diameter ⌀ mm red		60 −0,010/−0,020 (2.362″ −0.0004/−0.0008)	
blue		60 −0,020/−0,029 (2.362″ −0.0008/−0.000114)	
First undersize mm red		59,75 −0,010/−0,020 (2.352″ −0.0004/−0.0008)	
blue		59,75 −0,020/−0,029 (2.352″ −0.0008/−0.000114)	
Second undersize mm red		59,50 −0,010/−0,020 (2.342″ −0.0004/−0.0008)	
blue		59,50 −0,020/−0,029 (2.342″ −0.0008/−0.000114)	
Bearing material diameter mm		2,5 +0,003/−0,009 (0.0984″ +0.00012/−0.00036)	
First undersize mm		2,75 +0,003/−0,009 (0.108″ +0.00012/−0.00036)	
Second undersize mm		3,00 +0,003/−0,009 (0.118″ +0.00012/−0.00036)	
Main bearing clearance mm		0,029 ÷ 0,091 (0.0011″ ÷ 0.004″)	
Crankshaft journal diameter for alternator bearing ⌀ mm		35 +0,025/+0,009 (1.377″ +0.001/+0.00036)	
Bore diameter for alternator bearing in timing case cover ⌀ mm		62 −0,009/−0,039 (2.44″ −0.00036/−0.00156)	
Bore diameter for rear main bearing in engine housing ⌀ mm		65 +0,019/0 (2.56″ +0.00076/0)	

Engine

Specifications

Type	R 50/5	R 60/5	R 75/5
Bore diameter for front main bearing in main bearing retainer ⌀ mm		65 $^{+0,019}_{0}$ (2.56" $^{+0.00076}_{0}$)	
Connecting rod journal diameter ⌀ mm		48 $^{-0,009}_{-0,025}$ (1.89" $^{-0.00036}_{-0.001}$)	
Connecting rod journal diameter select fit oversize mm		48 $^{-0,034}_{-0,050}$ (1.89" $^{-0.00136}_{-0.002}$)	
First undersize mm		47,75 $^{-0,009}_{-0,025}$ (1.88" $^{-0.00036}_{-0.001}$)	
Second undersize mm		47,50 $^{-0,009}_{-0,025}$ (1.87" $^{-0.00036}_{-0.001}$)	
Connecting rod journal width mm		22 $^{+0,149}_{+0,065}$ (0.866" $^{+0.0595}_{+0.0026}$)	
Maximum allowable dynamic unbalance of crankshaft without flywheel cmp		20	
Crankshaft end play mm		0,08 ÷ 0,15 (0.0032" ÷ 0.06")	
Maximum allowable runout of front crankshaft stub measured with supported at the main bearing journals mm		0,02 (0.0008")	
Maximum allowable wear mm		÷ 0,20 (0.08")	
thrust washer red mm		2,483 ÷ 2,530 (0.098" ÷ 0.0995")	
thrust washer blue mm		2,530 ÷ 2,578 (0.0995" ÷ 0.1015")	
thrust washer green mm		2,578 ÷ 2,626 (0.1015" ÷ 0.103")	
thrust washer yellow mm		2,626 ÷ 2,673 (0.103" ÷ 0.105")	
Maximum flywheel clutch fall runout mm		0,10 (0.004")	
Connecting rod:			
Full length measured from center big end to center small end mm		135 (5.314")	
Connecting rod diameter at wrist pin mm		24 $^{+0,021}_{0}$ (0.945" $^{+0.00084}_{0}$)	
Connecting rod bushing bore ⌀ mm		22 $^{+0,020}_{+0,015}$ (0.866" $^{+0.0008}_{+0.0006}$)	
Connecting rod bushing bore ⌀ mm		22 + 0,040 (0.866" + 0.0015)	
Wrist pin bushing outer diameter mm		24,060 ÷ 24,100 (0.946" ÷ 0.948")	

Specifications

Engine

Type	R 50/5	R 60/5	R 75/5
Bore of connecting rod at big end ⌀ mm		$52 \, {}^{+0,010}_{0}$ ($2.047'' \, {}^{+0.0004}_{0}$)	
Bearing insert thickness Standard mm		1,983 ÷ 1,993 (0.078" ÷ 0.0785")	
Select fit undersize mm		1,995 ÷ 2,005 (0.0785" ÷ 0.0789")	
1st undersize mm		2,108 ÷ 2,118 (0.083" ÷ 0.0834")	
2nd undersize mm		2,233 ÷ 2,243 (0.088" ÷ 0.0885")	
Clearance desired mm		0,023 ÷ 0,069 (0.00092" ÷ 0.00276")	
Maximum allowable alignment deviation of connecting rod with bearing inserts installed mm		0,04 (0.0016")	
Maximum allowable torsion deviation of conrod bores mm		0,015 (0.006")	
Permitted weight difference between two connecting rods g		± 3 (± 0.105 oz.)	
Cylinder:			
Standard bore diameter A mm	67,00 (2.637")	73,50 (2.893")	82,00 (3.228")
B mm	67,01	73,51	82,01
C mm	67,02	73,52	82,02
1st oversize + 0,50 mm A	67,50 (2.657")	74,00 (2.913")	82,50 (3.248")
B	67,51	74,01	82,51
C	67,52	74,02	82,52
2nd oversize + 1,0 mm A	68,00 (2.677")	74,50 (2.933")	83,00 (3.267")
B	68,01	74,51	83,01
C	68,02	74,52	83,02
Cylinder surface finish		2,5 ÷ 4μm (0.0001" ÷ 0.00016")	

Specifications

Engine		R 50/5	R 60/5	R 75/5
Type				
Maximum allowable cylinder bore out-of round mm			0,01 (0.0004")	
Maximum allowable taper of cylinder bore			0,01 (0.0004")	
Maximum allowable wear of cylinder & piston mm			0,12 (0.0048")	
Piston:				
Piston shape			Convex — oval — pitched	
Weight selection			+ or — indicated	
Wrist pin selection			W or S indicated	
Standard piston diameter ⌀ mm	A B C	66,960 (2.63") 66,970 66,980	73,460 (2.89") 73,470 73,480	81,960 (3.22") 81,970 81,980
1st oversize + 0,50 mm (0.02")	A B C	67,460 (2.65") 67,470 67,480	73,960 (2.91") 73,970 73,980	82,460 (3.25") 82,470 82,480
2nd oversize + 1,0 mm (0.04")	A B C	67,960 (2.67") 67,970 67,980	74,460 (2.93") 74,470 74,480	82,960 (3.27") 82,970 82,980
Piston clearance mm			0,035÷0,045 (0.0014"÷0.0018") 0,035÷0,055 (0.0018"÷0.0022")	
Indication of direction of installation of piston			Arrow with the marking „vorn" (front)	

Specifications

Engine

Type	R 50/5	R 60/5	R 75/5
Piston rings:			
1st groove (Top ring)[1] height mm		$1.75 \, {}^{+0.060}_{+0.040}$ ($0.0689'' \, {}^{+0.0024}_{+0.0016}$)	
Ring gap mm	0,25÷0,40 (0.01"÷0.016")	0,25÷40 (dto)	0,30÷0,45 (0.012"÷0.018")
Side clearance mm		0,06÷0,07 (0.0024"÷0.0028")	
2"ND GROOVE (nose ring)[1] height mm		$2.00 \, {}^{+0.050}_{+0.030}$ ($0.08'' \, {}^{+0.002}_{+0.0012}$)	
Ring gap mm	0,25÷0,40 (0.01"÷0.016")	0,25÷0,40 (dto)	0,30÷0,45 (0.012"÷0.018")
Side play mm		0,05÷0,06 (0.002"÷0.0024")	
3rd groove (oil scraper ring)[1] height mm		$4.00 \, {}^{+0.030}_{+0.010}$ ($0.16'' \, {}^{+0.0012}_{+0.0004}$)	
Ring gap mm	0,20÷0,35 (0.008"÷0.014")	0,20÷0,35 (dto)	0,25÷0,40 (0.01"÷0.016")
Side play mm		0,03÷0,04 (0.0012"÷0.0016")	
Direction of installation		Writing on ring toward top	
[1]) Not according to German industrial, standards (DIN), BMW's own design			
Wrist pin:			
Wrist pin offset mm		1,5 (0.06")	

8. 69

Engine

Specifications

Type	R 50/5	R 60/5	R 75/5
Wrist pin diameter ⌀ Paint identification white mm		$22\,{}^{0}_{-0,003}$ (0.866" $\,{}^{0}_{-0.00012}$)	
Wrist pin diameter ⌀ Paint identification black mm		$22\,{}^{-0,003}_{-0,006}$ (0.866" $\,{}^{+0.00012}_{-0.00024}$)	
Wrist pin bore diameter in piston ⌀ When piston is identified With a „W" (white) On piston head		$22\,{}^{+0,003}_{0}$ (0.866" $\,{}^{-0.00012}_{0}$)	
Wrist pin bore diameter when ⌀ Piston is identified „S" (schwarz-black) In Piston head		$22\,{}^{-0,003}_{0}$ (0.866" $\,{}^{+0.00012}_{0}$)	
Wrist pin clearance 1. in piston mm		0,000÷0,006 (÷0,00024)	
Clearance of wrist pin In wrist pin bushing Identification white		0,015÷0,023 (0.0006"÷0.00092")	
Identification black		0,018÷0,026 (0.00072"÷0.00104")	

1. Piston and wrist pin should be replaced together

Specifications

Engine

Type			R 50/5	R 60/5	R 75/5
Top speed			The actually achieved maximum speed of a broken-in motorcycle depends to a large extend to the wind resistance offered by the rider due to his size, posture and clothing, and on road and weather conditions		
Sitting upright	km/h	(mph)	ca. 145 (92)	ca. 155 (98)	ca. 165 (108)
Chrouched	km/h	(mph)	ca. 157 (100)	ca. 167 (105)	ca. 175 (115)
Acceleration from 0 to 30 mph	in seconds		3,0	2,6	2,2
from 0 to 40 mph	in seconds		4,0	3,5	2,8
from 0 to 50 mph	in seconds		6,6	5,5	4,1
from 0 to 60 mph	in seconds		10,2	8,2	6,4
from 0 to 80 mph	in seconds		14,8	11,3	9,5
from 0 to 90 mph	in seconds		22,7	17,0	12,7
from 0 to 100 mph	in seconds			28,0	19,8
¹/₄ mile	in seconds		17,2	15,8	14,6
Standing kilometer	in seconds		32,3	30,4	28,2
Average attained speed	km/h	(mph)	111 (66.6)	118 (70.8)	128 (76.8)

Torque specifications mkp (ft/lbs)

Cylinder head nuts 1,5÷3,5÷3,5 (10.8÷25.3÷25.3)
Connecting rod bolts 3,5÷3,9 (25.3÷28.2)
Flywheel bolts 4,8÷5,2 (34.7÷37.6)
  5,8÷6,2 (41.9÷44.8)

Oil pan 1,2 (8.7)
lock nut on valve
adjustment 1,8÷2,2 (13.0÷15.9)

All other screws and nuts should be tightened following the usual normal values quoted in the tables of the screw firms or in the new BMW standards sheet 60002.1

11 00 050 Engine removal and installation

Remove transmission 23 00 020

Remove fuel tank 16 11 030

Remove left ignition coil 12 13 010

Remove exhaust system 18 00 020

Remove right carburetor
Unscrew two allen head bolts and remove upper engine cover (starter cover)

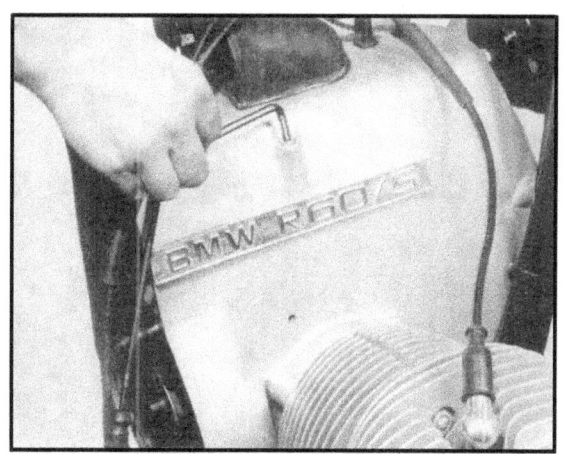

Disconnect starter cable

Loosen upper horn mounting bolt. Unscrew the three allen head bolts and remove front engine cover

Fitting instruction:

When installing, be sure that the ventilating hose is firstly installed into the engine protection cover.

Unplug cable from alternator
(1 = DF, 2 = D-top)
Unplug wire from condensor

Unscrew hex. head bolt with lock nut (4) and pull out tachometer cable

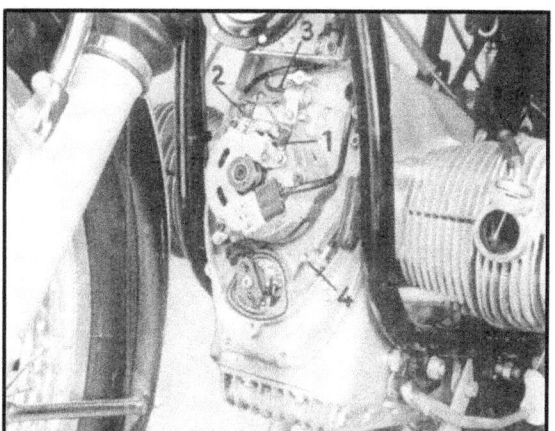

Unplug the two wires from the diode chassis (arrow)

■

Unplug the wire on the left side of the diode chassis (arrow)

■

Remove left and right ignition wires an unplug wire from the oil pressure sensing switch (5)

■

Withdraw front and rear engine through bolts

Assembly instructions; before inserting the front engine through bolt, place the center stand brackets between the engine housing and the frame on both sides. In addition the side stand bracket is placed between engine and frame on the left side.

The rear engine through-bolt holds the foot rests and the exhaust pipe clamps. **Attention,** a spacer is required between the engine housing and the frame at the rear through-bolt.

■

Remove engine to the left, tilt engine slightly to the left and downward to facilitate removal.

Install the engine on work stand BMW No. 6000 in device BMW No. 6005/1 and fasten by screws. Prior to disassembling the engine, it's good practice to check ignition timing 12 11 004, contact breaker points gap 12 11 141 as well as the value clearances 11 34 504 in order to localize previously existing faults and to hold them in mind on further checks.

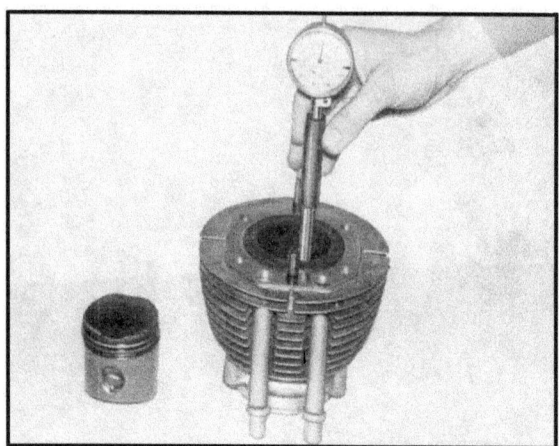

11 11 527 Cylinder boring and honing

11 12 100 Cylinder head removal and installation
11 25 500 Piston removal and installation

The preparatory steps explained heretofore should be accomplished only if necessary.

The cylinders can be bored to two oversizes 0.020" (0,5 mm) and 0.040" (1,0 mm). Boring to a 3rd oversize is not allowed.

Measure bored and honed cylinder and select the proper size piston. For correct clearance see 'Specifications'.
Install new cylinder; measure cylinder, select correct piston for proper clearance.

∎

Leaking of the pushrod seals can be eliminated by driving the pushrod tubes inward. BMW tool No. 221

∎

11 12 100 Cylinder head removal and installation

Remove cap nut and the two nuts on each end of the valve cover.
Remove rocker box cover and gasket.

Remove the four (4) shoulder nuts and withdraw the rocker arms and push rods.

Install two shoulder nuts diagonally across on two cylinder through bolts. Install bracket BMW tool No. 209. Withdraw cylinder and cylinder head by tightening cap nut (hex. size 14 mm) on rocker box cover center bolt. As soon as the cylinder is free of the engine housing, remove the two nuts (hex. size 14 mm-see arrow) and separate cylinder from cylinder head with a light mallet blow. Withdraw cylinder head and cylinder from through bolts.

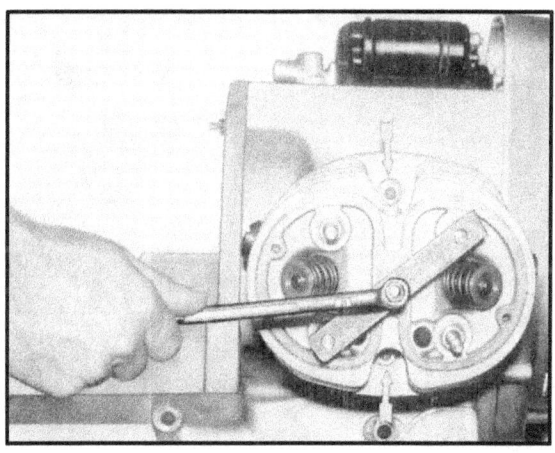

Assembly instructions: First place rocker arm alignment tool, BMW tool No. 200, on rocker arms. Tighten the six cylinder head nuts in the following sequence.
1st to 11 ft/lbs
2nd to 18 ft/lbs
3rd to 25 ft/lbs

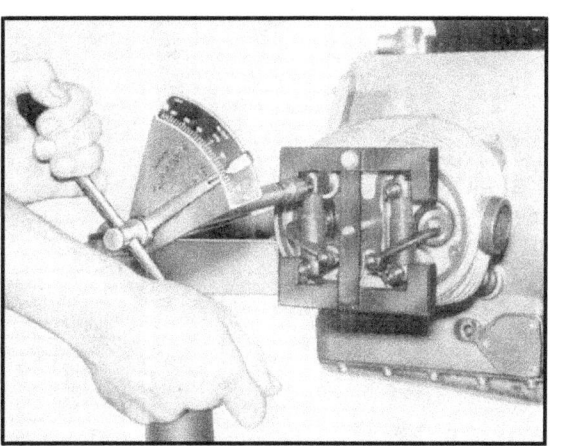

See chart (Specifications)

11 12 503 Cylinder head disassembly and reassembly and valve grinding

Cylinder head removed according to 11 12 100

Mount cylinder head on fixture, BMW tool No. 5034, clamp the fixture into a vise. Compress the valve springs with the compressor lever of tool 5034. Remove the valve keepers, spring retainers, and valve springs. Remove cylinder head from holder and remove both valves.

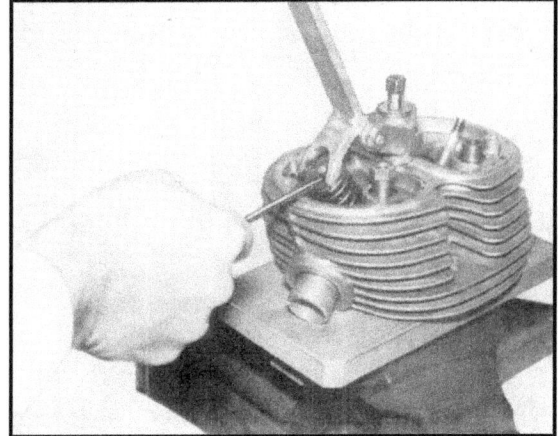

Inspection of cylinder head:

Check a) for cracks and good gasket surfaces.
       b) tightness of valve guides and valve seats.
       c) valve guide wear.
       d) valve stem and rocker arm pads for wear.
       e) rocker arm clearance.
       f) valve springs for specified length and tension (see 'Specifications')

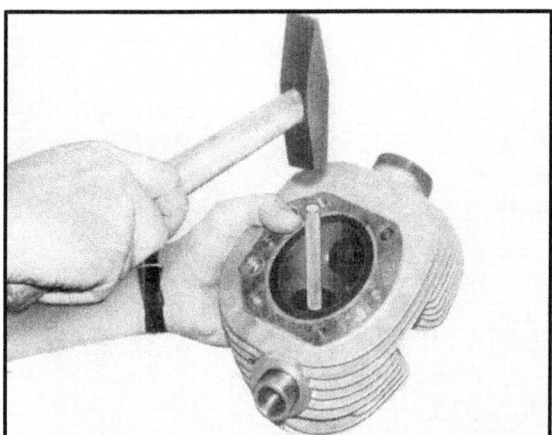

Refacing valve seats: Reface the valve seats in the cylinder head with the "Hunger" or another suitable seat refacer. The valve seat face has an angle of 45° 20'. The seat width is 1,5 mm (0.060") for the intake valve and 2,0 mm (0.080") for the exhaust valve, measured at a 45° angle. Chamfering toward the combustion chamber should be 15°, chamfering toward intake or exhaust port should be 75°. The seat at the valve should be positioned near the outer diameter.

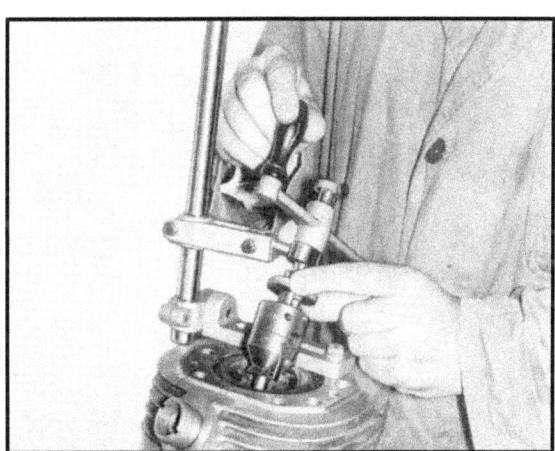

Reface valves on a valve grinder to an angle of 45° 20'. Inspect the margin (edge) after the valves are refaced. Valves with less than 1 mm (0.040") margin should be replaced. Refaced valves and recut valve seats using the "Hunger" valve seat cutter do not have to be lapped. Check tight seating of valves by filling the intake (exhaust) port with gasoline. Check for leaking gasoline.

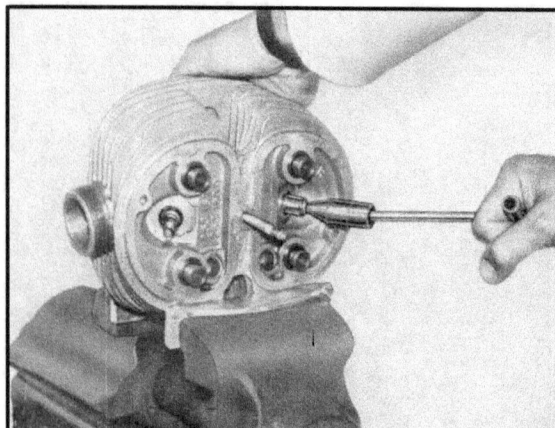

If necessary lap in valves using holder, BMW tool No. 540.

11 12 561 Valve guide replacement

Cylinder head removed according to 11 12 100.
Cylinder head disassembled, reassembled, and valves ground according to 11 12 503.
The preparatory steps explained heretofore should be performed only if necessary.
Machine valve guides down to the snap ring.

Remove snap ring, heat cylinder head to 360° F and drive valve guides toward combustion damper using drift, BMW tool No. 5128.

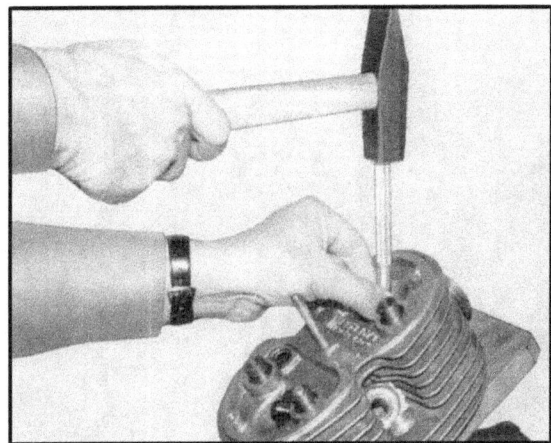

Install snap rings on new valve guides and press valve guides into heated cylinder head. (For fit see "Specifications"). Let cylinder heads cool down and ream valve guides with reamer 8H7.

11 12 621 Valve Seat Replacement

Valve seats have to be replaced after several refacings. Machine off valve seat without damaging the seat bore. Use a "Hunger" valve seat cutter or other suitable tool. Heat the cylinder head to 450°—500° F and install new valve seats. (For fit see "Spezifications").

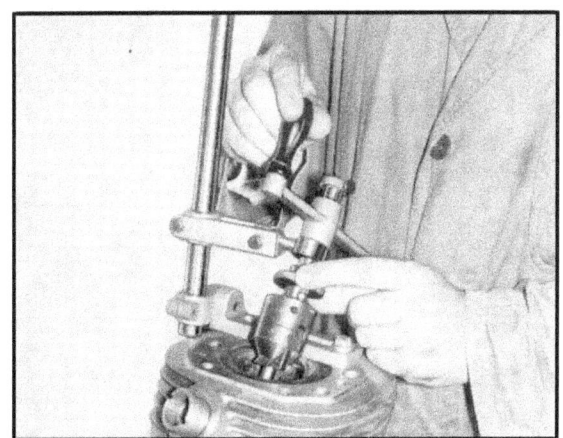

8. 69

11 14 800 Timing case cover removal and installation

Engine is removed according to 11 00 050.
Alternator removed and installed according to 12 31 212
Automatic timing advance removed and installed according to 12 11 141.
Remove the nine allenhead bolts and three allennuts with an allen wrench.

■

Install the puller, BMW tool No. 214, into the altenator mounting holes. **Caution:** install the insert into the crankshaft.

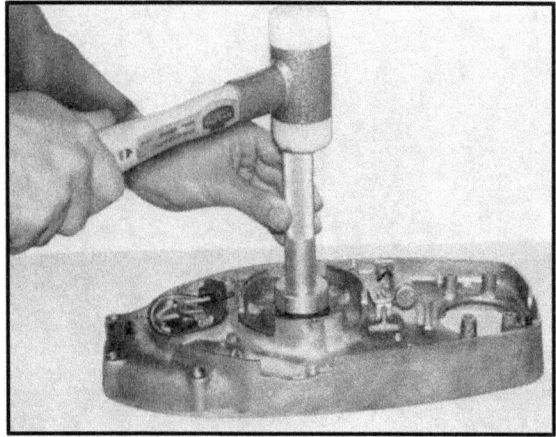

■

Replace defective seals. To install crankshaft seal use drift, BMW tool No. 224.

■

If the seal of the tachometer pinion has to be replaced proceed as follows: Remove clamp bolt, withdraw bushing, drive tachometer pinion out using a soft metal drift. The seal will come out with the pinion.

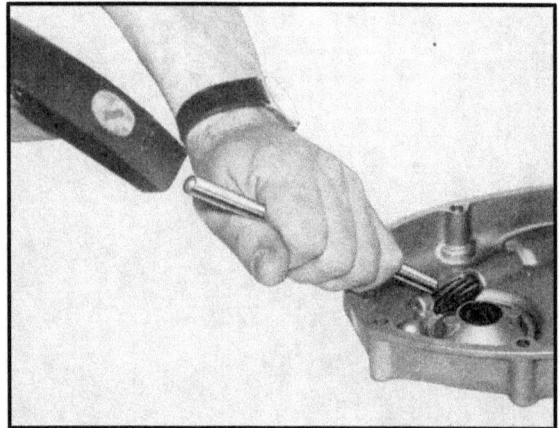

■

Install tachometer pinion, seal and bushing, tap in with suitable drift.

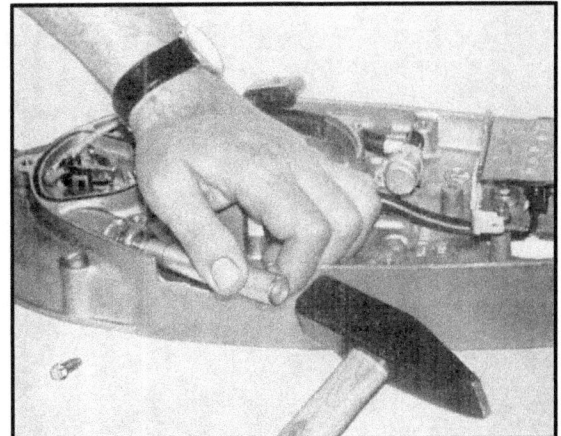

Installing timing case cover. Place crankcase in horizontal position. Lay gasket, and two sealwashers (arrow) on crankcase.
Before installing cover remove diode chassis and seal for advance unit shaft. Heat cover to 180°.

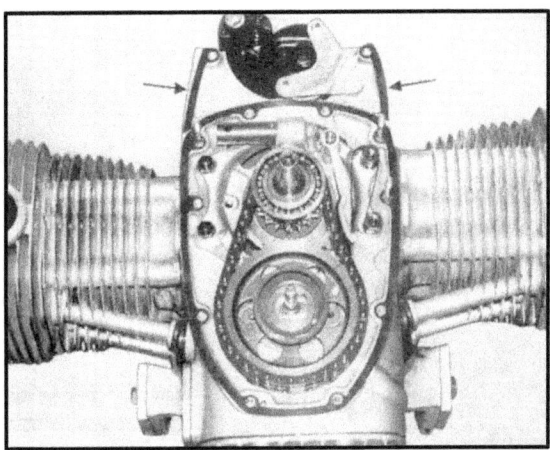

Install guide bushing, BMW tool Nr. 225, into seal bore for advance unit shaft. Install timing case cover. Install allenhead bolts and nuts and tighten starting from the center to both sides.

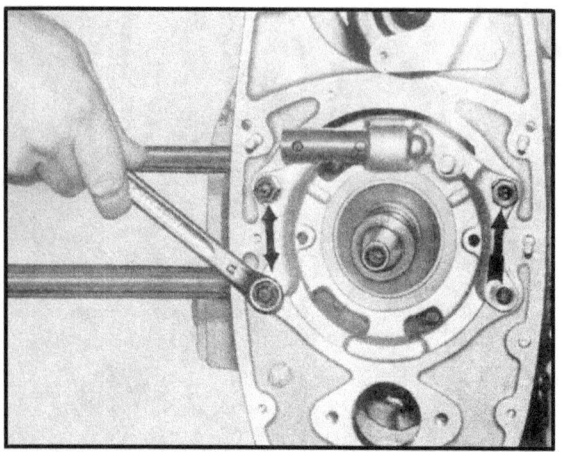

11 21 501 Crankshaft replacement

Engine removed according to 11 00 050.
Cylinder head removed and installed according to 11 12 100
Connecting rod removed and installed according to 11 24 500
Piston removed and installed according to 11 25 500
Timing sprockets replaced according to 11 31 061
Oil pump removed and installed according to 11 41 500
Alternator removed and installed according to 12 31 212
Clutch removed and installed according to 21 21 500
The preperatory steps explained heretofore should be performed only if necessary.
Remove remaining three hex. nuts and one shoulder nut (hex. size 14 mm), and two nuts (hex. size 13 mm) from main bearing retainer.

■

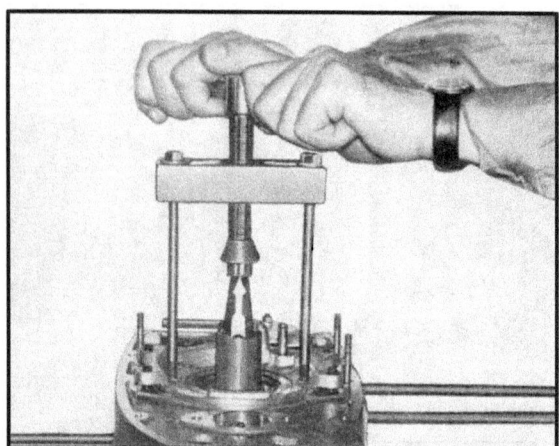

Install two bolts from puller, BMW tool No. 216, into the holes provided in the bearing retainer. Put insert into crankshaft and place puller (same as Kukko puller No. 6026 M8) parallel to the bearing retainer. Pull bearing retainer off.

■

Turn crankshaft until front counter weight is even with the upper recess. Remove crankshaft.

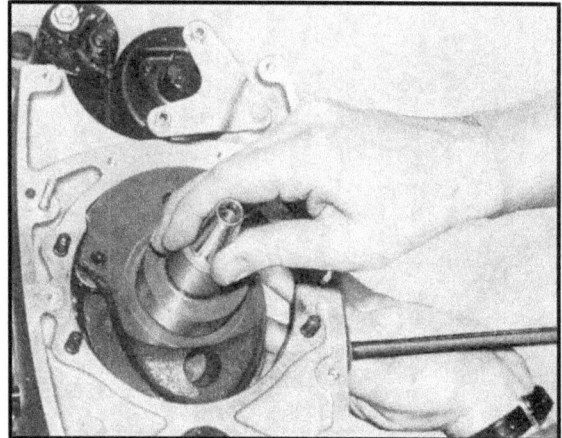

■

Remove both thrust rings from the two locating pins using drift, BMW tool No. 219.

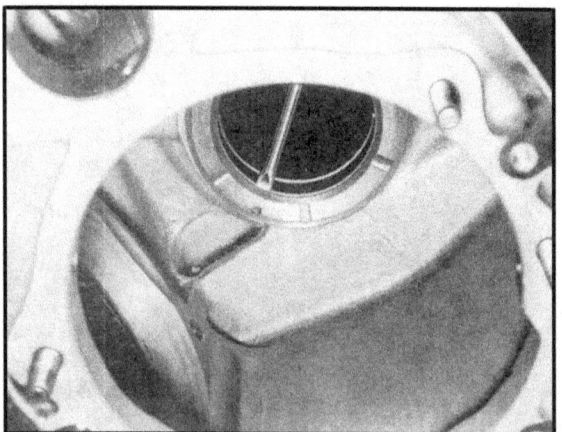

■

Measure crankshaft and insert bearings.

Remove housing from repair stand.
Measure main and connecting rod journals with a micrometer horizontally and vertically.

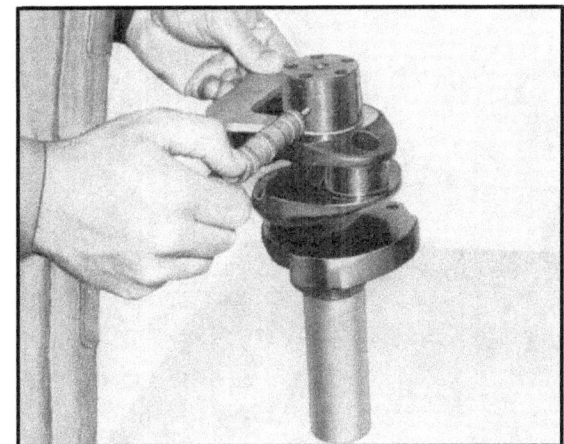

Insert in crank case.

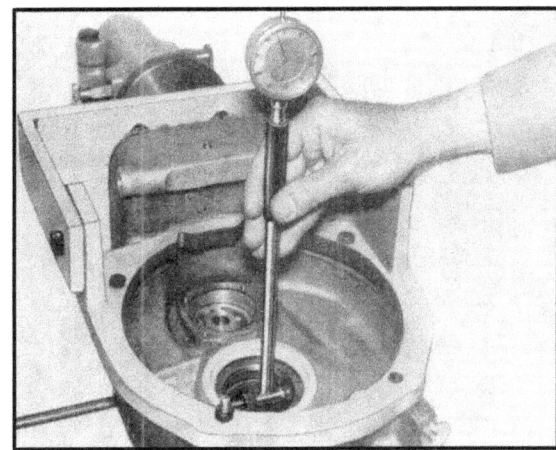

Front main bearing retainer.

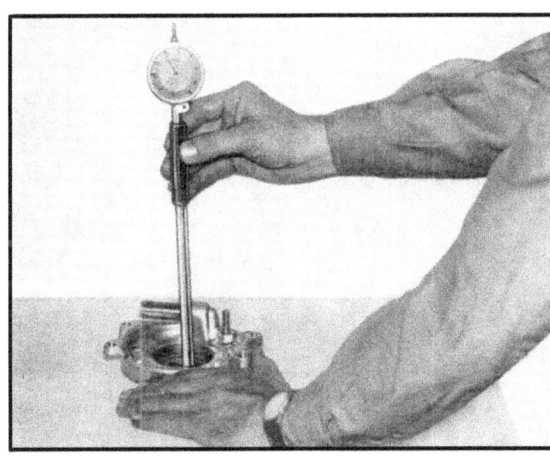

Bolt connecting rod caps and connecting rods together and measure in two positions using an inside micrometer. (For data see 'Specifications')

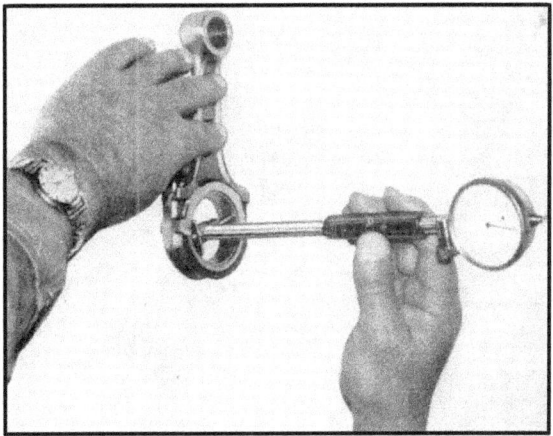

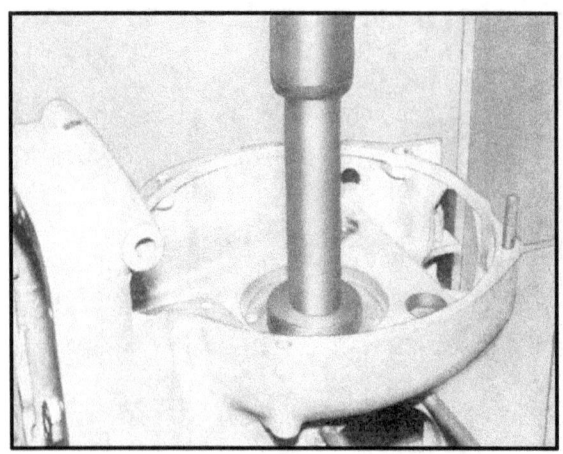

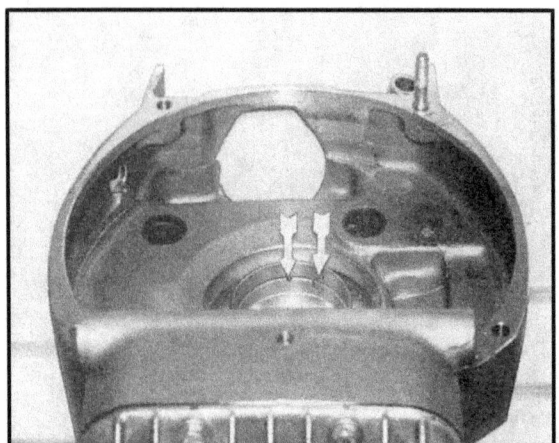

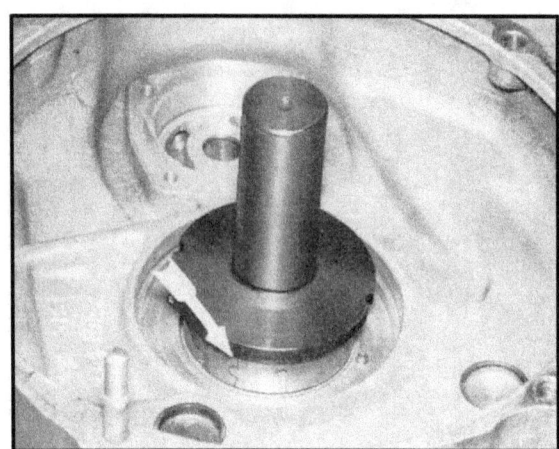

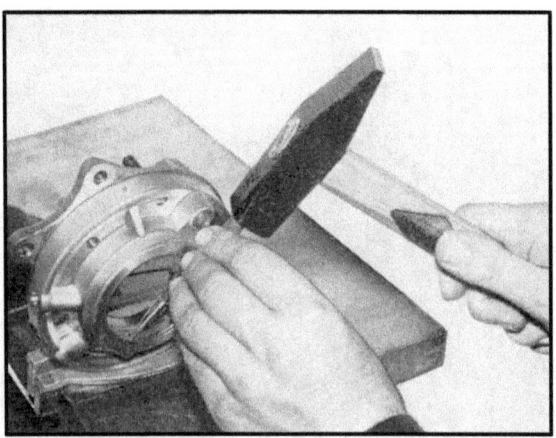

11 21 531 Main bearing insert replacement

Engine removed according to 11 00 050
Cylinder head removed and installed according to 11 12 100
Connecting rod removed and installed according to 11 24 500
Piston removed and installed according to 11 25 500
Timing sprockets replaced according to 11 31 061
Oil pump removed and installed according to 11 41 500
Alternator removed and installed according to 12 31 212
Clutch removed and installed according to 21 21 500

The preperatory steps explained heretofore should be performed only if necessary.

Heat engine housing to 180—200°, place it over the sleeve, BMW tool No. 205. The pins of the inner thrust washer have to fit into the holes provided in the sleeve. Press bearing insert out using the removal mandrel of BMW tool No. 205.

∎

Installation of the 1st or 2nd oversize bearing inserts.

Heat engine housing to 180—200 F.
Place aluminum block of fixture BMW tool No. 205 on the removal sleeve. Place engine housing on fixture so that both pins fit into the holes provided in the aluminum block. Insert bearing, position the bearing joint 26° to the right of top center as viewed from the rear, with the oil holes being exactly vertical.

∎

Put installation mandrel with fiber bushing into bearing insert and press bearing insert into housing.
Caution: the mandrel is provided with two cutouts which fit over the locating pins. The width of the bearing insert provides for a slight recess on both sides.

∎

Replacing bearing insert in main bearing retainer.

Drive location pin out from the inside with a drift.
Heat cover to 180—200° F. Place it on the cylinder of fixture, BMW tool No. 205. Press it out with removal mandrel of fixture, BMW tool No. 205.

∎

Heat bearing retainer to 180—200° F.
Place new bearing insert into retainer. The bearing joint should be positioned 26° left of top center as viewed from the front with the oil holes exactly vertical.

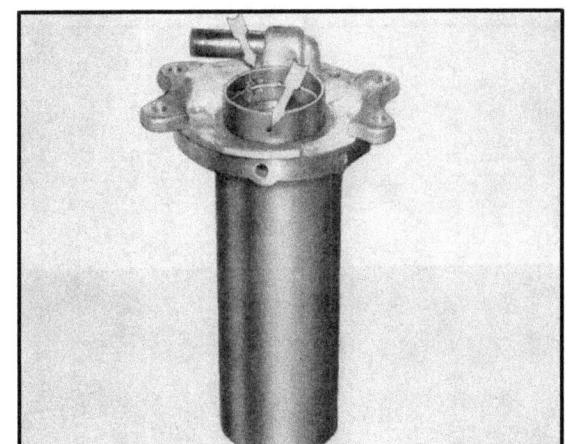

Clamp bearing retainer into vise (use jaw protectors). Drill two (0.126") holes into the bearing insert through the existing passages in the retainer. Carefully deburr holes in the insert.

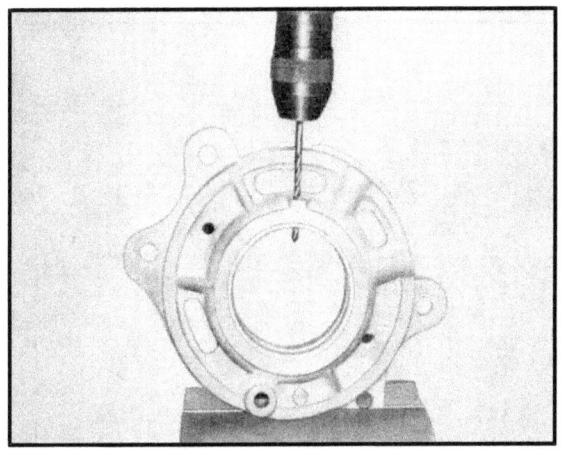

Locking bearing insert.
Start a hole in the bearing insert using a drill 0.153" (exact size of locating pin hole) through the locating pin hole (position 3). Finish the hole with a 0.150" drill. Ream the hole with a hand reamer 4H8. Do not ream completely through. This provides a blind hole and prevents the locating pin from passing through the bearing.

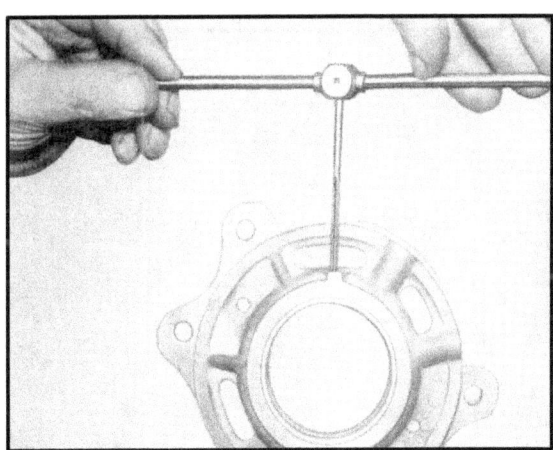

Clamp installation mandrel with fiber sleeve into vise. Put cover over mandrel and tap in locating pin far enough that it recedes 0.02÷0.04" from the inner bearing surface. Centerpunch pin in place and carefully deburr hole.

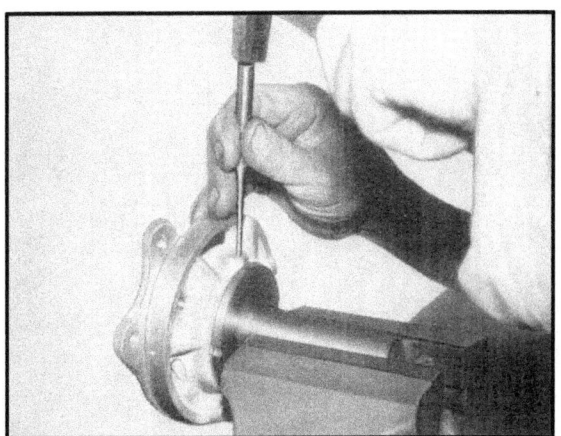

Adjusting end-play of the crankshaft

Size chart of thrust washers.

Max. thickness mm		Color
2,483÷2,530	0.098" ÷0.0995"	red
2,530÷2,578	0.0995"÷0.1015"	blue
2,578÷2,626	0.1015"÷0.103"	green
2,626÷2,673	0.103" ÷0.105"	yellow

To adjust end-play of crankshaft, install two thrust washers on the locating pins: a green marked washer inside, and a red marked one outside.

Both locating pins should protrude the same distance on both sides: Heat the engine housing for installation and possible correction of location of the pins.

■

Heat engine housing to 180° F. Mount the housing in the repair stand and place it vertically. Carefully insert crankshaft. Turn housing horizontal and install front main bearing retainer and tighten it. Turn engine 180° and install flywheel according to 11 22 510.

■

Turn engine to bring crankshaft into a horizontal plane and install dial indicator on clutch housing. Determine end-play, remove flywheel and measure thrust washer (red) with micrometer.
Use dial indicator, and holder BMW tool No. 5104.

■

Example

Actual end play	0,18 mm	0.00709"
desired end play	0,12 mm	0.00472"
difference	0,06 mm	0.00237"
thickness of washer removed	2,48 mm	0.09763"
add	0,06 mm	0.00237"
thrust washer should be	2,54 mm	0.10"

Select a blue thrust washer which is as close to the desired thickness as possible. The thickness should not be more than plus 0,03 mm (0.0012") or minus 0,04 mm (0.0016") of the desired thickness. Install chosen thrust washer on the locating pins.

Install new crankshaft seal using drift, BMW tool No. 201. Tap seal completely home. Oil the seal lightly and install flywheel. (For torque see "specifications").

11 22 510 Flywheel removal and installation

First method
With engine removed; engine removed according to 11 00 050. The pictures and text explain the procedure to follow with the engine removed.

Second method
With transmission removed. Transmission removal according to 23 00 020
(Engine remains in frame)
Clutch removal and installation 21 21 500

Install holder, BMW tool No. 292, on the flywheel. Holder lays against gussets in clutch housing.

■

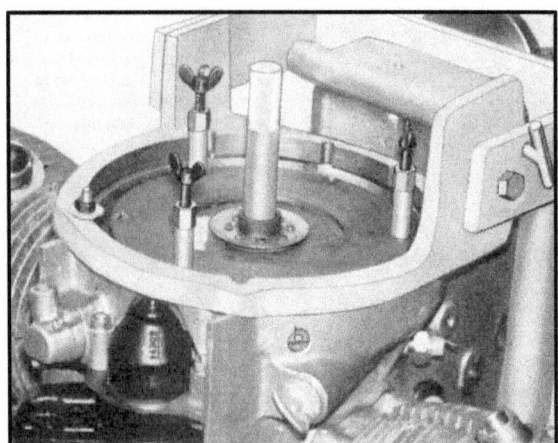

Remove the five flywheel bolts. Screw two clutch compression bolts, BMW tool No. 534, into flywheel and carefully lift flywheel out without cocking it.

■

To reassemble, set piston to top dead center, line up the OT mark of the flywheel in the inspection hole. Install the five flywheel bolts, mount the flywheel holder, BMW tool No. 292, (for torque see "specifications"). The flywheel bolts are expansion head bolts and have to be installed dry.

■

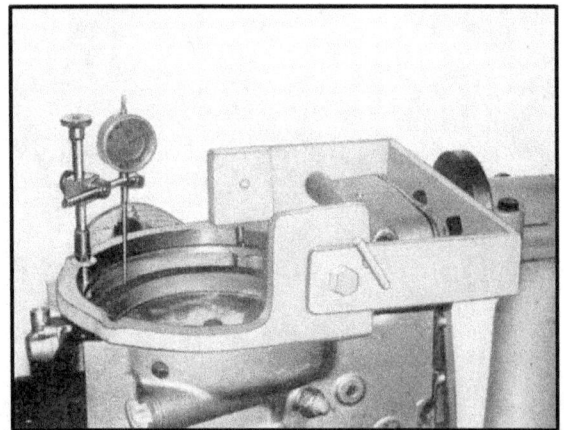

Check clutch face runout of the flywheel with dial indicator using holder, BMW tool No. 5104.
Place the engine vertical for checking of the runout. (To check runout with engine installed push against center of crankshaft to prevent it from moving back.)

■

11 24 500 Connecting rod removal and installation

engine removed	according to 11 00 050
cylinder head removed	according to 11 12 100
piston removed and installed	according to 11 25 500

The preparatory steps explained heretofore should be performed only if necessary.

To remove and install the connecting rod, turn the crankshaft to top dead center. Remove connecting rod bolts with a serrated socket, insert M10. Withdraw connecting rod and rod cap with bearings.

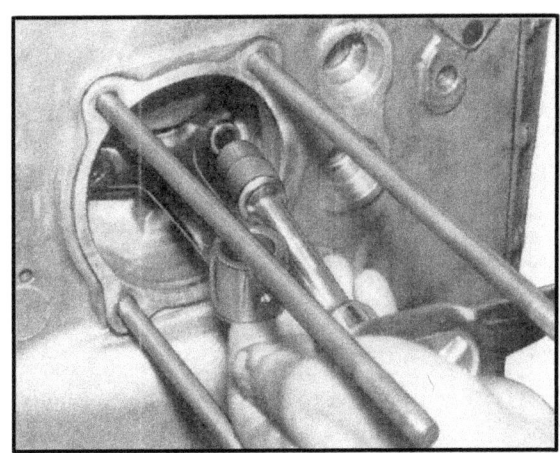

Assembly instructions: When installing the connecting rods place the locating pins on both rods forward.

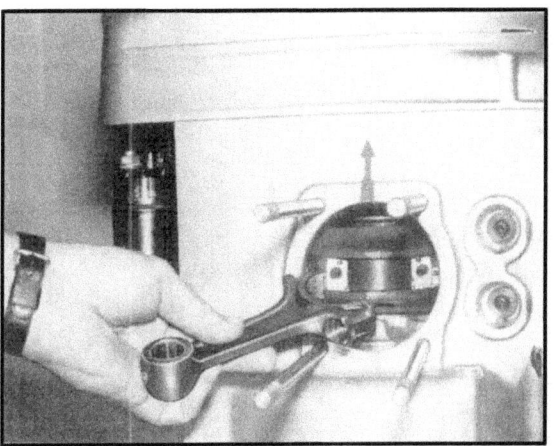

Inspection and repair. Measure connecting rod big end with a micrometer.

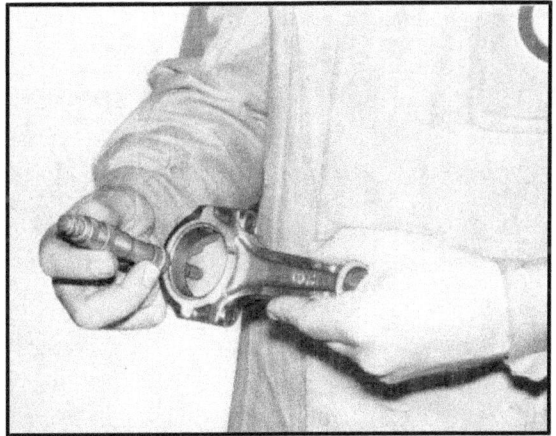

Check wrist pin bushing for tightness in the connecting rod, and check wrist pin for proper fit in the bushing. If the wrist pin has too much play in the bushing, replace the bushing.

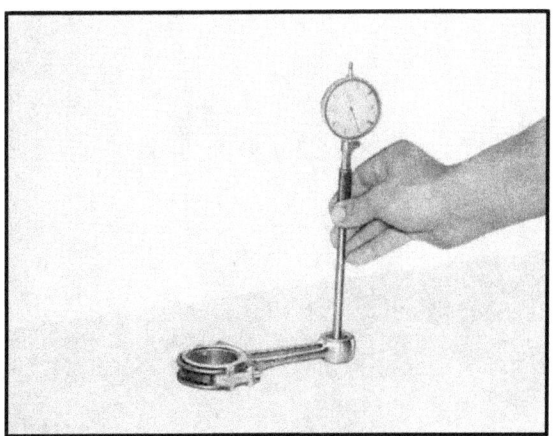

Press new wrist pin bushing in. Mount connecting rod in a lathe and turn bushing to a high finish to the proper size. (See Specifications)

■

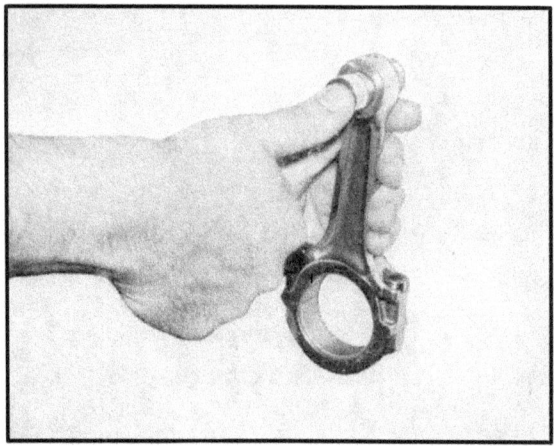

A correctly fitting wrist pin can be pushed through the bushing with light thumb pressure.

■

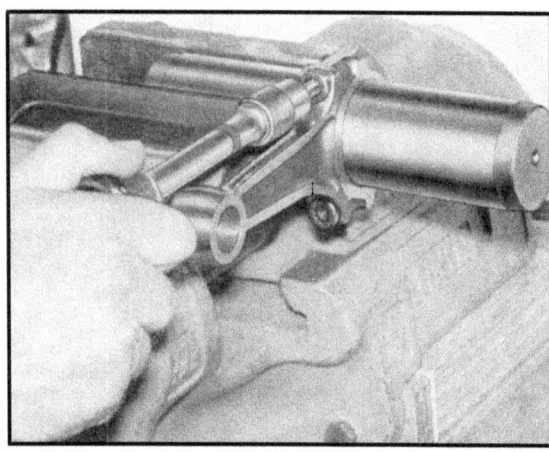

Measuring and straightening of connecting rods; Install a set of inserts into the big end (a set of inserts should be kept on hand to be used for this check whenever it is done) and mount the rod on a hardened ground mandrel. The rod should have no clearance on the mandrel. Insert a pin 150 mm (5.91") long, which fits without play, through the wrist pin eye.

■

Lay two exactly alike prisms on a surface plate, place connecting rod vertical and measure the distance from the plate to the top of the pin at the wrist pin eye, to see if big end bore and wrist pin eye are parallel.

■

Clamp connecting rod into vise for straightening. (Use jaw protectors). (For allowable deviation with the use of a 150 mm (5.91") pin see Specifications).

Check connecting rod for twist.

Place two prisms on the surface plate support wrist pin eye on the surface plates that the distance from the plate to the centerline of the connecting rod and wrist pin eye is approx the same. Check with dial indicator on the big end mandrel and wrist pin to check for twist. If necessary straighten (for allowable deviation see Specifications).

11 24 551 Replacing connecting rod inserts

Push inserts into clean connecting rod.

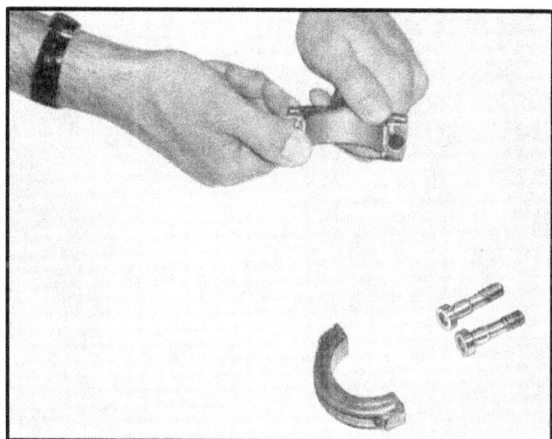

Before installation of the crankshaft, coat main and rod inserts with Molykote Paste "G".

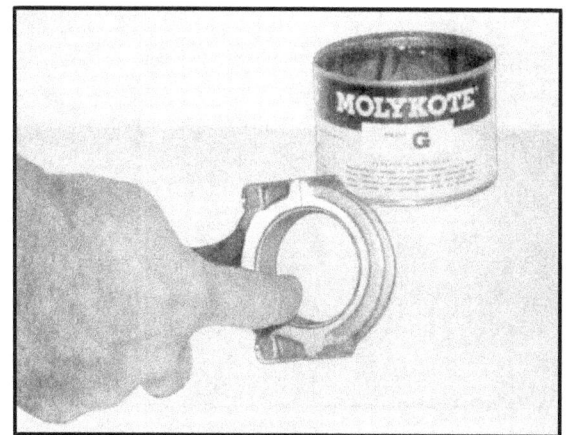

11 25 500 Piston removal and installation

Cylinder head removed and installed according to
11 12 100

Withdraw cylinder and base gasket from through bolts.
Caution: insert wooden protection fixture under piston
skirts before withdrawing the cylinder completely to prevent damage to the pistons.

■

Remove wrist pin lock ring with an awl or a small screw driver, remove wristpin with drift, BMW tool No. 210.

■

Assembly instruction:

The marking "vorn→" should point forward, this is important since the wrist pin is off center.
The piston does not have to be heated for wrist pin installation.

■

Position the circlip in the groove so that one end overlaps the opening. Press on center of circlip using drift, BMW tool No. 210.

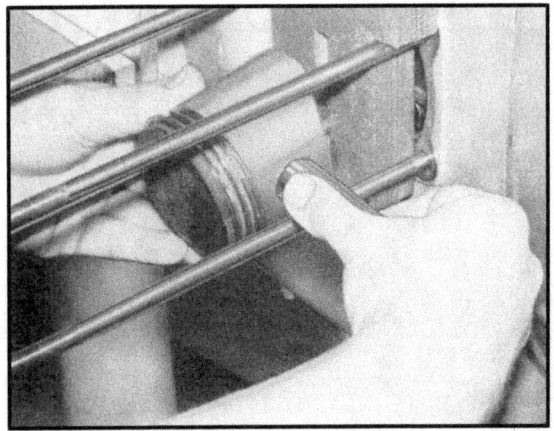

■

Inspection and repair, measure cylinders horizontally and vertically approximately 10 mm (0.4") from the top, in the middle and near the bottom with an inside micrometer at an ambient temperature of approx. 68° F.

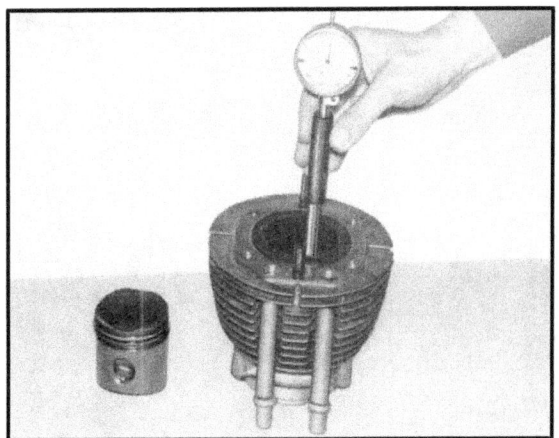

Measure piston at the piston skirt crosswise to the wrist pin bore.

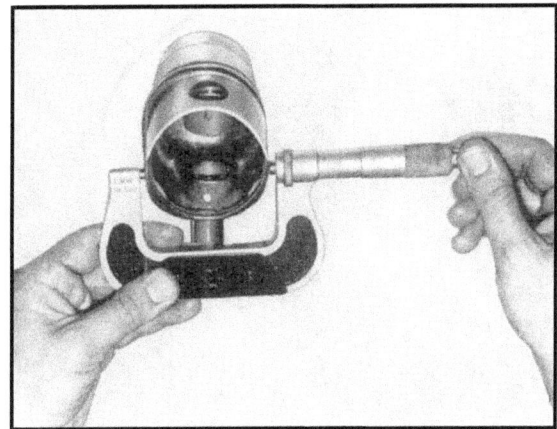

Measure piston ring clearance and end gap with a feeler gauge.
(For cylinder wear data, piston size and ring clearance and gap see "Specifications".)

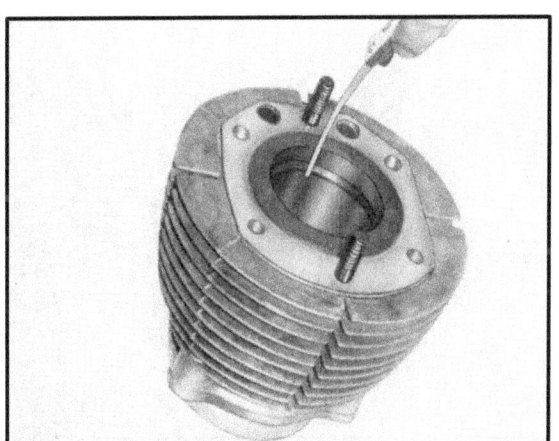

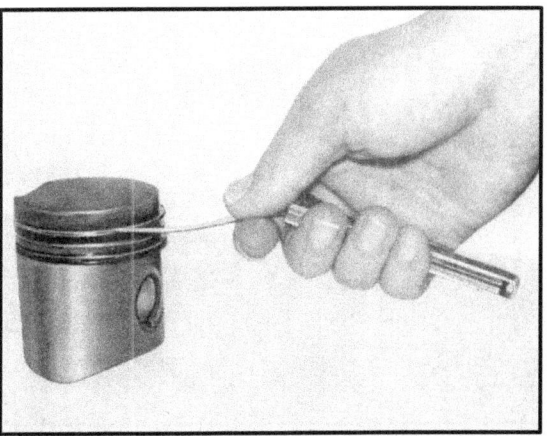

11 31 061 Timing sprockets replacement

Engine removed according to 11 00 050
Alternator removed and installed according to 12 31 212

Place crankcase horizontal, install puller insert into crankshaft and install puller BMW tool No. 217 and remove ball bearing.

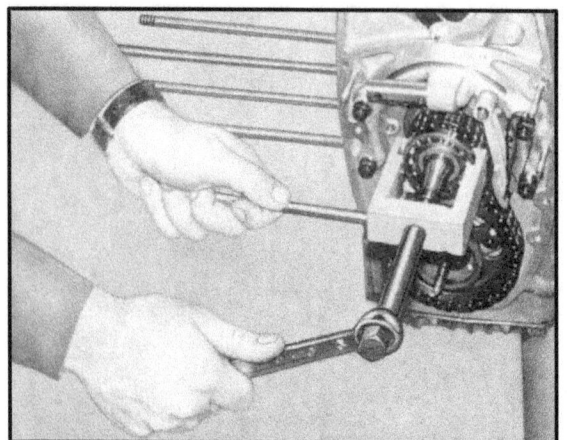

■

Remove the two phillips screws holding the front camshaft bearing with a recessed phillips screw driver.

■

Remove circlip, chain tensioner, and tensioner spring.

■

Place puller insert in end of crankshaft and install sprocket puller, BMW tool No. 213. Pull off crankshaft sprocket, follow up evenly with camshaft.

■

Place camshaft on an anvil tube (approximate tube dimensions-inside diameter 90 mm [3.54"], outside diameter 106 mm [4.17"], length 225 mm [8.86"]) so that sprocket lies flat, place sleeve BMW tool No. 212 on camshaft and press off sprocket together with tachometer drive gear.

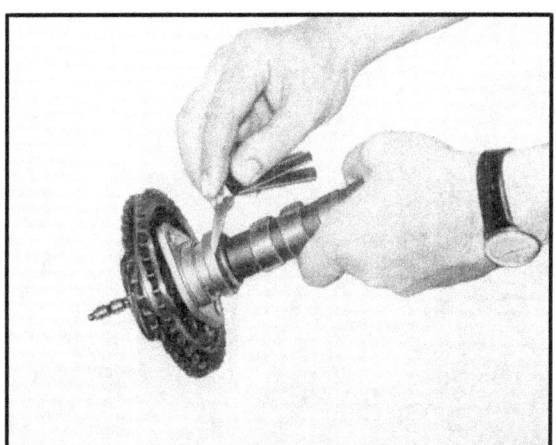

Before reinstalling the sprockets, coat the inside bore lightly with tallow. If the chain has stretched and has to be replaced, it is good practice to also replace the camshaft and crankshaft sprockets.

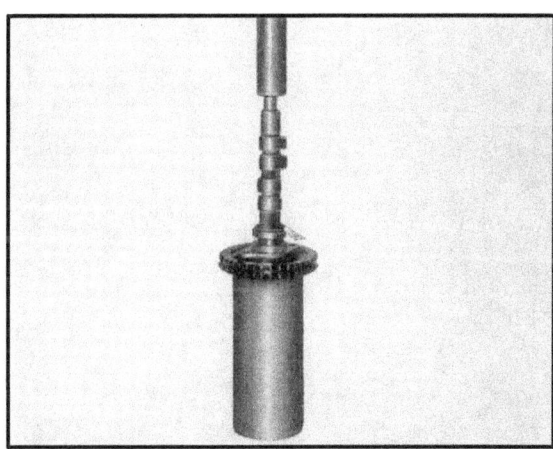

Checking end-play of camshaft. The assembly of the camshaft is in reverse order of the disassembly. Insert front camshaft bearing on camshaft, press on camshaft sprocket first and then press on tachometer drive gear, check end-play between camshaft bearing and camshaft with a feeler gauge. (For clearance see "Specifications".)

To install the camshaft, place engine housing vertical. Insert camshaft and crankshaft sprocket into chain, line up markings in the center.

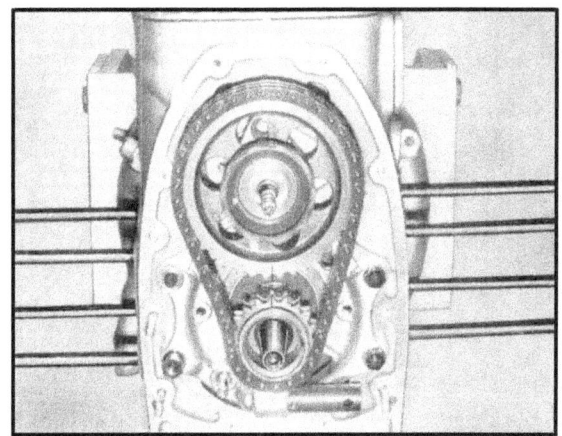

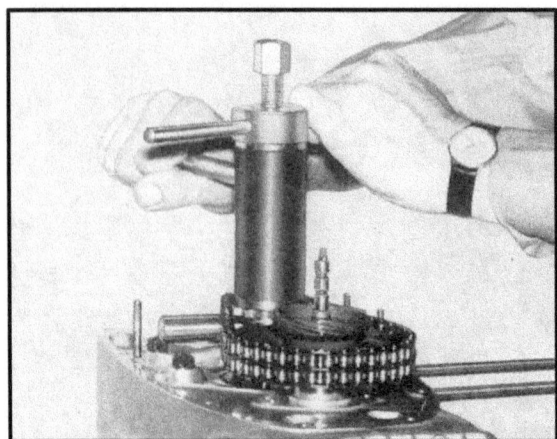

Insert camshaft into engine housing — push crankshaft sprocket on crankshaft carefully so that key and key groove mate. Install fixture sleeve, BMW tool No. 216, and puller bolt, BMW tool No. 535, over sprocket into the end of the cranshaft and pull the sprocket on.
Caution — guide camshaft into its rear bearing bore.

■

Tighten front camshaft bearing with two phillips head screws.
Heat ball bearing to 170°F and install. Install chain tensioner and tensioner spring, do not deform spring. Check contact surface of chain tensioner.

■

11 34 504 Adjusting Valve Clearance

Loosen acorn nut and the two nuts (arrow), remove rocker cover and gasket.

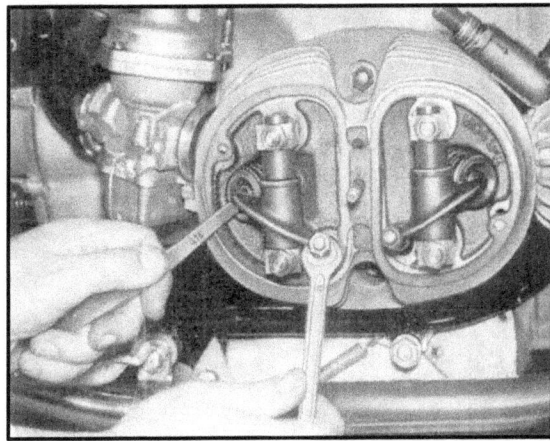

Adjust valve clearance with feeler gage between valve stem and rocker arm when engine is stopped and cold. To do this, unscrew spark plugs and turn engine over with cranked screw driver at the alternator rotor bolt until the cylinder to be adjusted is at compression top dead center. Both valves are closed. If necessary, readjust the clearance at the adjuster screw after loosening the lock nut; secure with lock nut. Recheck valve clearance. Valve clearance see specifications.

11 41 500 Oilpump removal and installation

First method

With engine removed; engine removal according to 11 00 050.

The pictures and text explain the procedure to be followed with the engine removed.

Second method

With transmission removed; transmission removal according to 23 00 020.

Engine remains in frame.

Clutch removed and installed according to 21 21 500.

Flywheel removed and installed according to 11 22 510.

Remove the 4 countersunk screws and remove oil pump cover.

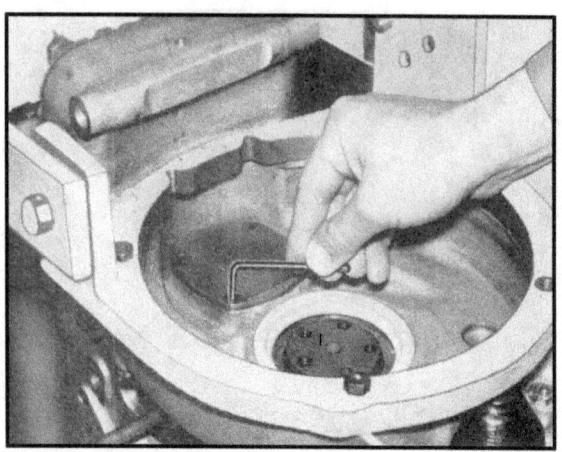

■

Pull out inner and outer pump rotor.

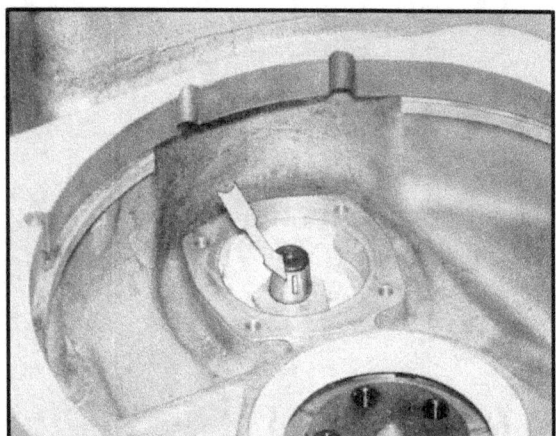

■

Remove woodruff key. Stuff a rag into the openings to prevent the key from falling in before attempting the key removal.

■

Inspection. Check clearance between housing and outer pump rotor.

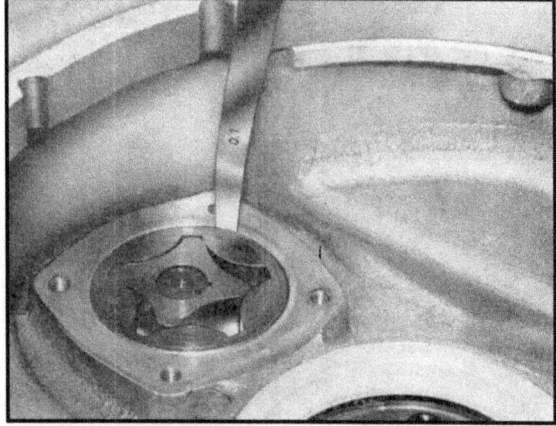

■

Check clearance over rotor.

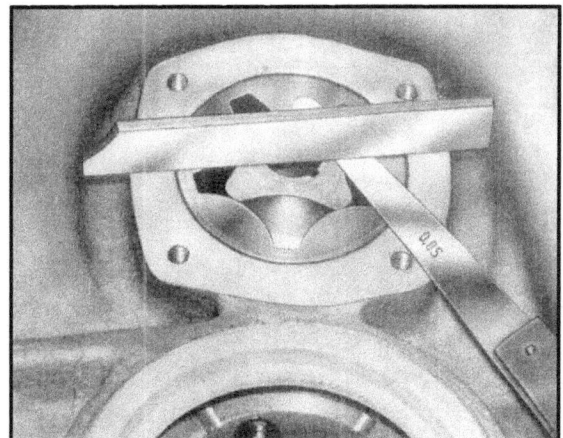

Check clearance between inner and outer rotor.
(for clearances see „Specifications")

To reassemble, install woodruff key and push on rotor, with the chamfer of the inner rotor toward the engine. Caution, it is good practice to always replace O-ring in cover.

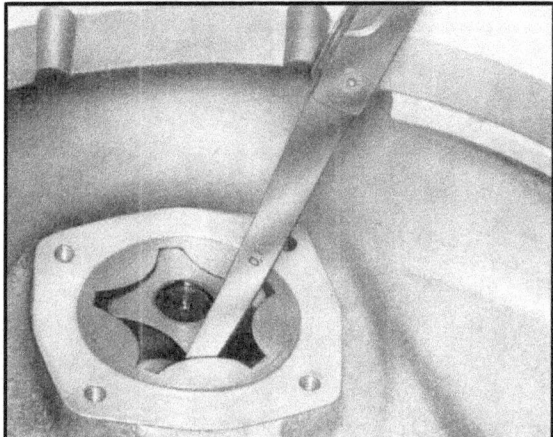

12 Engine electrical system

Specifications	. . . .	Page 3
12 11 004	Timing adjustment	7
12 11 141	Breaker points replacement	10
12 13 010	Ignition coil removal and installation	11
12 31 212	Alternator removal and installation	12
12 32 000	Regulator removal and installation	14
12 41 020	Starter removal and installation	15
12 41 170	Starter protection relay removal and installation	17

Specifications

Engine electrical system

	R 50/5	R 60/5	R 75/5
Type			
Starter:			
Type (Bosch)		DF 12 V 0,5 PS	
Amperage draw maximum Amp.		290	
Power output HP		0,5	
Torque mkp (lb-ft.)		0,885 (6.4)	
Protection relay		Stribel SR 9570	
Alternator:			
Type (Bosch)		Bosch G 1 14 V 13 A 19	
Drive of alternator		Mounted directly on crankshaft	
Maximum output W/V		180/14	
Maximum current output		13	
Charging begins at RPM		980	
Maximum RPM		10 000	
Max. allowable out-of-round on the slip rings mm		0,06 (0.0024")	
Max. diameter of the slip rings mm		26,8 (1.055")	
Regulator:			
Typ (Bosch)		AD 1/14 V	
Regulated voltage without load Volt		13,5 ÷ 14,2	
with load Volt		13,9 ÷ 14,8	

Specifications

Engine electrical system

	R 50/5	R 60/5	R 75/5
Type			
Diode carrier Type (Bosch)		0 197 002 001 RS 20/1 A 1 A	
Ignition coil: Type (Bosch)		E 6 V	
Starting spark length With 300 sparks/min. and 3 V. mm		8 (0.32")	
Operating spark length With 3,600 sparks/min. mm		13,5 (0.54")	
Spark plugs: Thread		M 14 × 1,25	
Bosch	W 230 T 30	W 230 T 30	W 200 T 30
Beru	230/14/3 A	230/14/3 A	200/13/3 A
Champion		N 7 Y	
Spark plug gap mm		0,7 (0.028")	
Ignition breaker: Type (Bosch)		Automatic timing advance mounted on camshaft	
Advance beginns		800	
Maximum advance at		2500	
Grease for advance unit and breaker cam		Bosch grease Ft 1 v 4	
Grease for breaker cam shaft		Bosch grease Ft 1 v 22 or Ft 1 v 26	
Breaker point gap		0,35—0,40 (0.014"—0.016")	
Breaker arm spring tension		450	

Specifications

Engine electrical system

Type	R 50/5	R 60/5	R 75/5
Dwell angle		110° ± 1°	
Condenser capacitance		0,2 μF — 25%	
Static timing adjustment (for engine assembly)		9° v OT	
Timing range		31° ± 2° 30'	

Torque Specifications mkp (ft/lbs)

Armature mounting bolt	2,3÷2,7 (16.6÷19.5)	
Starter motor mounting bolts	4,75 (34.3)	
Spark plugs		2,3÷3 (16.6÷21.7)

All other screws and nuts should be tightened following the usual normal values quoted in the tables of the screw firms or in the new BMW standards sheet 60002.1

8.69

12 11 004 Ignition timing

Loosen three allenhead bolts and remove front engine cover

Fitting instruction: When installing, be sure that the ventilating hose is firstly installed into front engine cover.

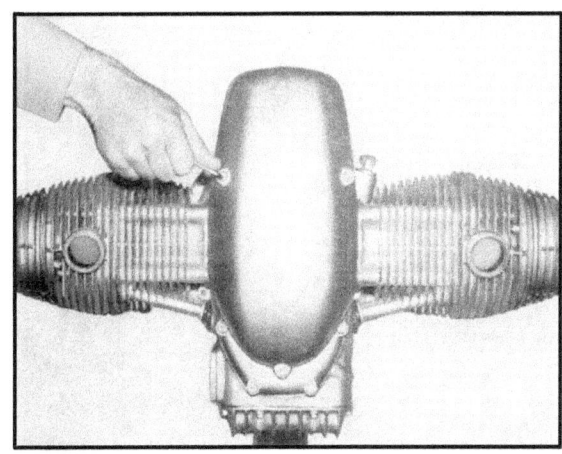

If no dwell meter is available proceed as follows: Remove spark plugs, insert an allen wrench into the armature mount bolt (allen wrench size 6 mm). Turn crankshaft clockwise (as seen viewed from the front).

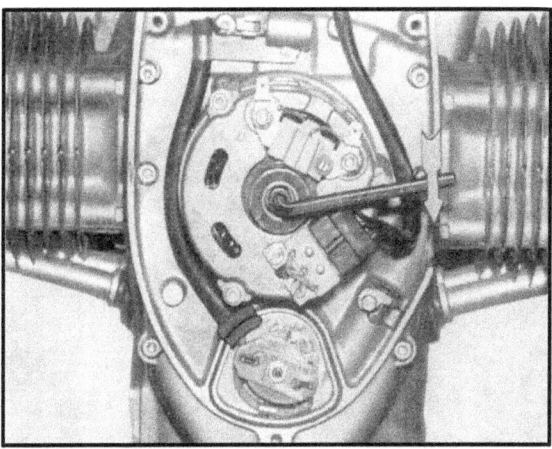

The breaker lever has to lift off fully. Check gap with feeler gauge. If necessary replace the breaker points. 12 11 141

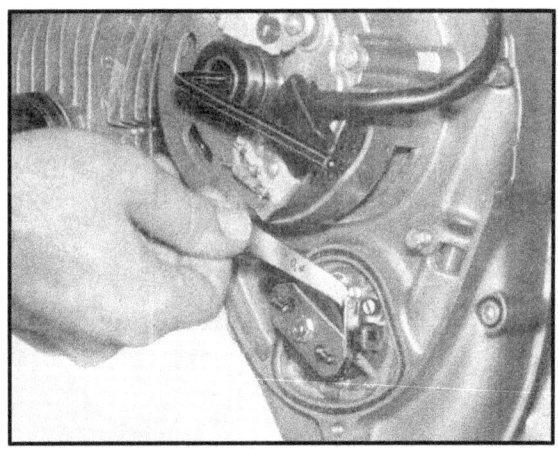

Adjusting the beaker point gap. Loosen locking screw (arrow), insert screw driver between the two pins and into the slot of the contact and adjust gap as required. Tighten the locking screw. Recheck dwell angle and recheck point gap.
(for dwell angle and point gap see "Specifications")

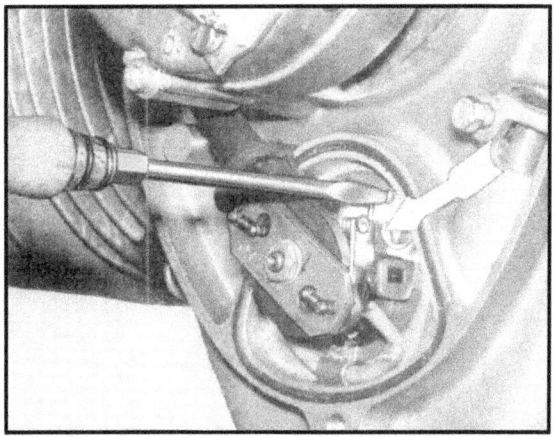

Ignition timing check

Engine removed or installed
Engine removed according to 11 00 050

a) with continuity light
b) with neon type timing light

a) Connect continuity light between condensor (1) and ground (2). Ignition turned on.

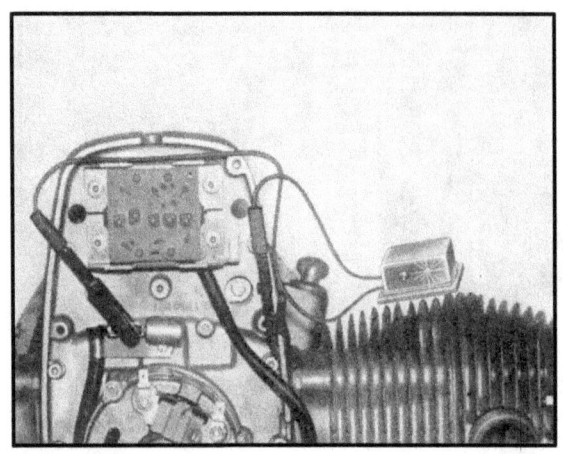

■

Turn engine clockwise (direction of rotation), Light must light up when the 'S' mark on the flywheel lines up with the marking in the engine housing. (advance unit flyweights retracted) Maximum allowable difference between left and right cylinder is 2°. This is 2 mm (0.08") if measured on the flywheel.

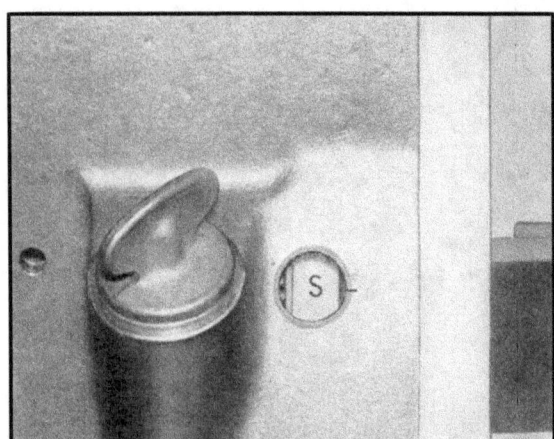

■

b) When checking the timing with a timing light connect the timing light to spark plug wire. Observe the position in the inspection hole with the engine running.

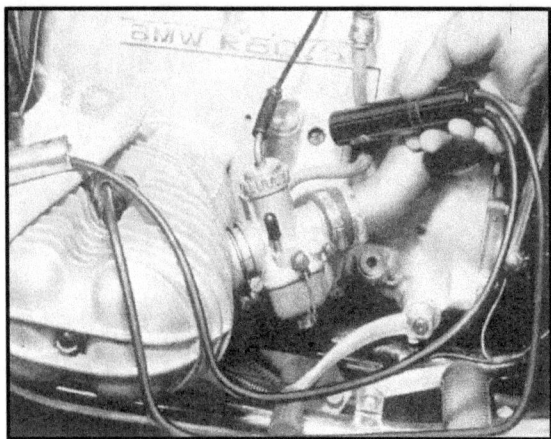

■

With the engine running at idle (800–1000 RPM) the 'S' mark (retarted or Slow) must appear as the white line in the inspection hole. If the line is above the center the ignition is too far advanced. If the line is below the center the ignition is too far retarded. As the RPM is increased the 'S' mark will disappear to the top (beginning of advance approximately 800 RPM) and the 'F' mark will appear from below ('F'-advanced or Fast) at approximately 2500 RPM. This signifies full advance.

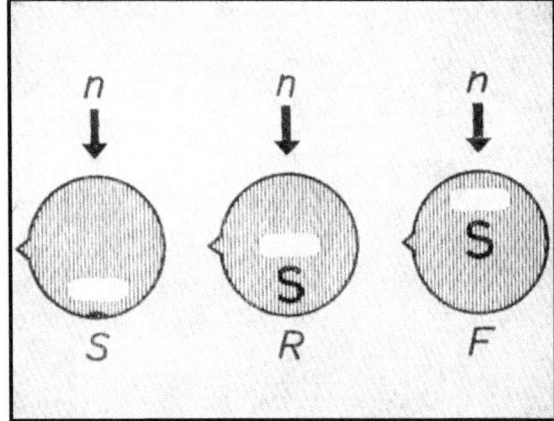

■

Adjusting the timing: Loosen the two screws that hold the point plate. Turning the plate in direction of rotation retards the timing, turning it against the direction of rotation advances the timing. (Crankshaft and camshaft turn in the same direction). After completing timing adjustment tighten the two screws.

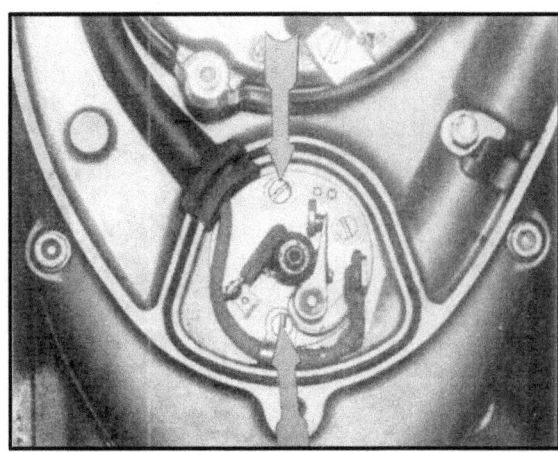

To adjust the timing with a continuity light, first turn the crankshaft 45° against the direction of rotation (light goes out), to take up any possible slack in the engine components. Now turn engine in the direction of rotation until light lights up. Adjust as necessary.

Recheck timing with a timing light. If the timing is incorrect check runout of shaft on camshaft, and check advance unit for ease of movement. Maximum allowable runout of shaft 0.02 mm (0.0008").

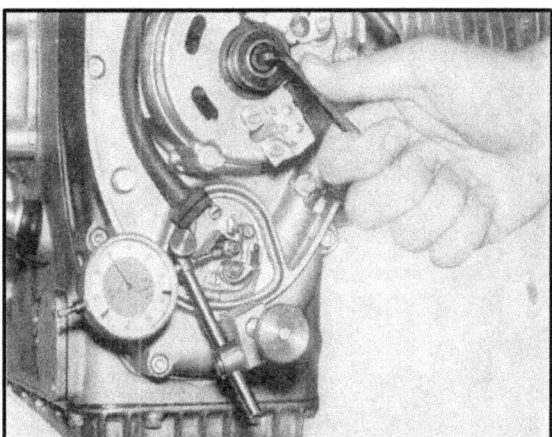

12 11 141 Replacing the breaker points

Loosen the three allenhead bolts and remove the front engine cover. Remove the hex. nut holding the advance unit and withdraw the advance unit. When reinstalling the advance unit align the locating nose.

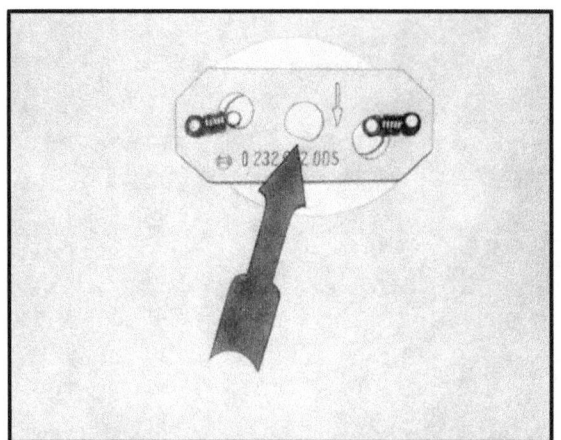

■

Check contacts for wear, in an emergency they can be cleaned but they should always be replaced. To remove the points, remove the fillister head screw (arrow), withdraw the wire from the condensor and remove the point plate.

■

During reassembly make certain that the brass axle for the breaker arm is inserted through the proper hole.

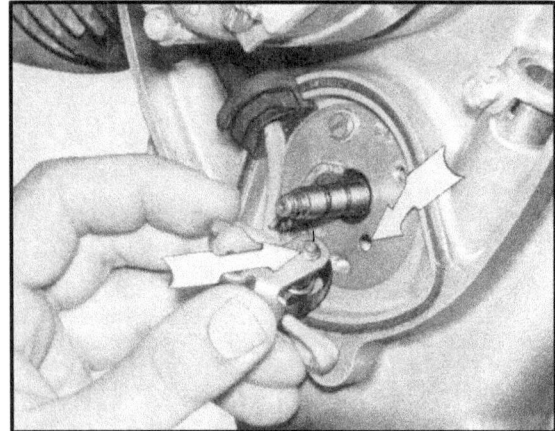

■

Before installation of the advance unit examine the felt for the breaker cam, if necessary apply a small amount of Bosch grease F t 1 v 4 to it. Apply a small amount of grease F t 1 v 22 on the advance unit axle. Check timing advance weights for ease of operation after installation.

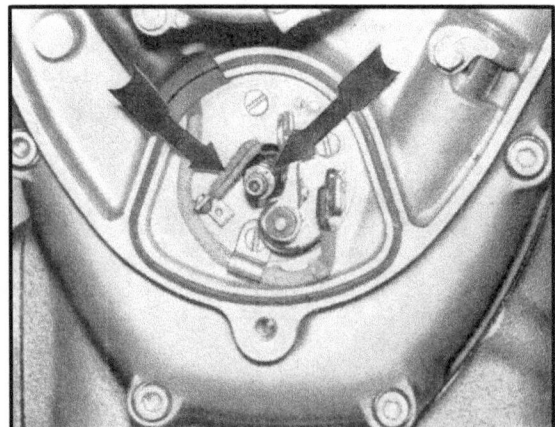

■

12 13 010 Ignition coil removal and installation

Remove fuel tank according to 16 11 030

Disconnect negative cable from battery

Disconnect wires from terminals '1' and '15' of the coil and disconnect high tension cable

Remove coil allen mounting bolts and remove coil

Assembly instruction: The front mounting bolt of the left coil is also used to hold a ground wire.

12 31 212 Alternator removal and installation

Engine removed according to 11 00 050
Remove the three allenhead bolts and remove the front engine cover

Fitting instruction: When installing, be sure that the ventilating hose is firstly installed into front engine cover.

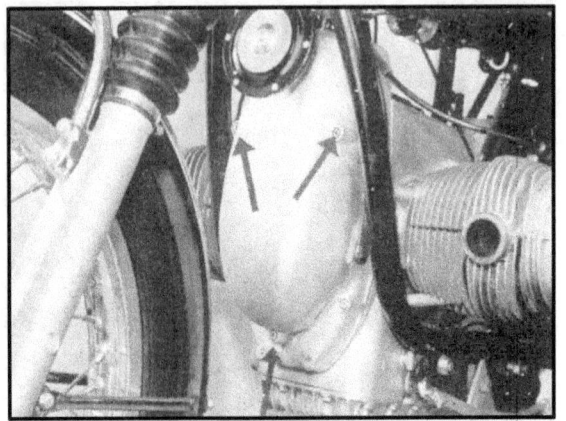

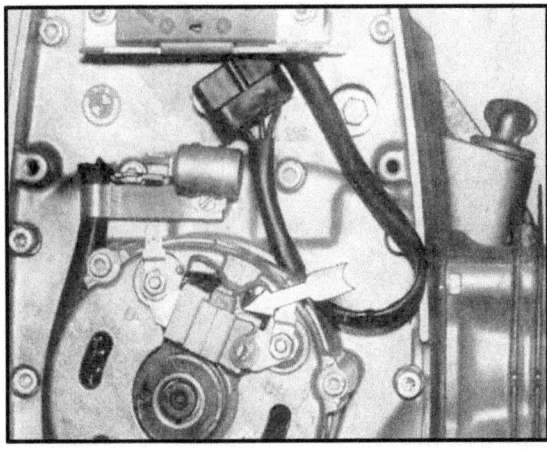

Unplug the three-prong plug from the alternator stator. Lift the brushes and clamp them in by placing the brush springs on the side of the brushes

Remove the three allenhead bolts from the stator housing

Remove the armature mounting bolt and press armature off with a puller bolt, BMW tool No. 5030.

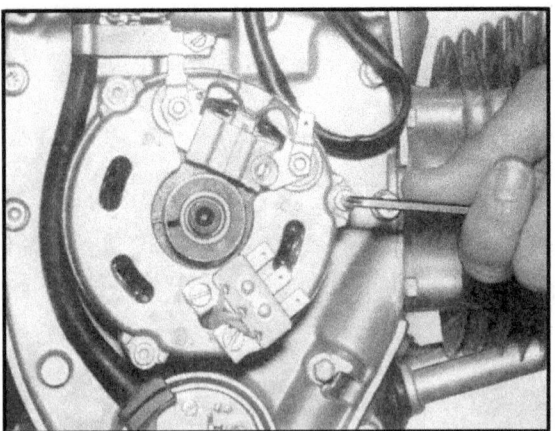

Repairing the alternator.

Remove the two nuts (hex. size 8 mm) from the inside of the stator housing. Withdraw brushholder with brushes. If the brushes have to be replaced, be careful during re-soldering so that no solder runs down into the brush wires. Install insulator bushing on the stud of the brush holder, install insulating washers and install brush holder into stator housing.

Scored slip rings have to be turned in a lathe to a high finish. Mounting taper should have no runout. (for maximum allowable runout and minimum slip ring diameter see 'Specification').

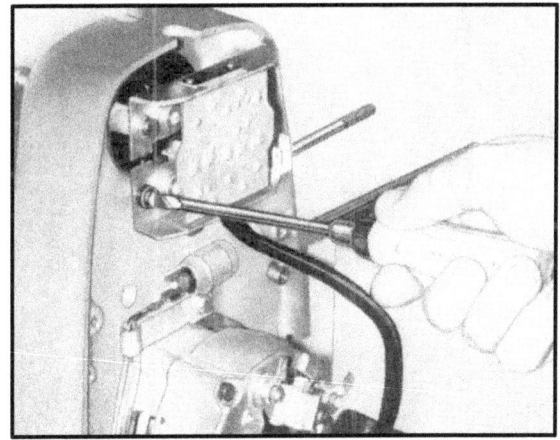

Diode chassis replacement.
Remove diode chassis. Withdraw plug, install new diode chassis connect three-prong plug.

12 32 000   Regulator renoval and installation

Fuel tank removal and installation 16 11 030

Disconnect negative battery cable. Withdraw connector (arrow). Remove the two phillips-head screws and remove the regulator.

12 41 020 Electric starter removal and installation

Remove micronic filter insert 13 72 000

Remove fuel tank 16 11 030

Loosen the three hose clamps of the right air tube, withdraw the rubber sleeve and remove the air tube.

Loosen hex.nut (1) and hex.head bolt (2) of the right air filter housing. Remove filter housing, withdraw breather hose to the rear.

Remove the two allenhead bolts on the left and right and remove upper engine (starter) cover.

Unhook the battery straps, remove battery cover and disconnect negative battery cable.

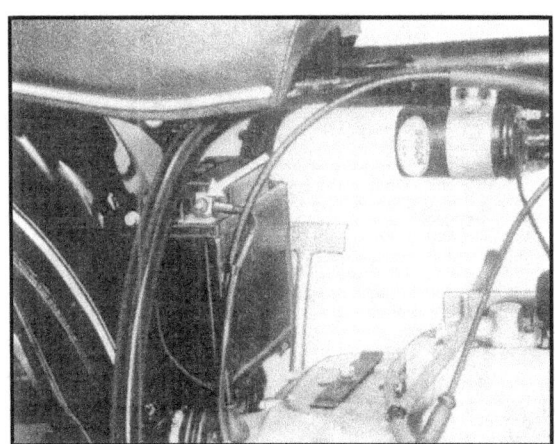

Disconnect starter cables.

■

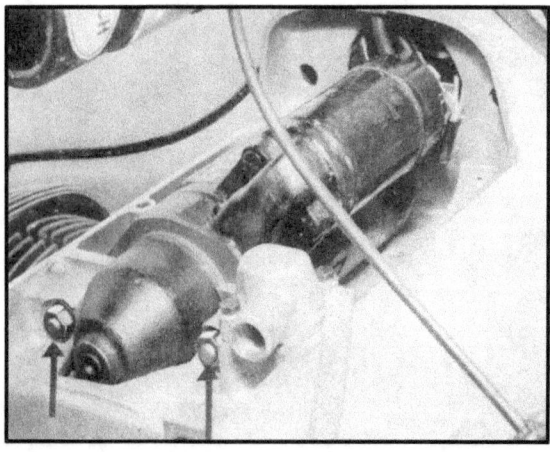

Remove rear mounting bolts (arrow).

■

Loosen upper horn mounting bolt.

Remove the three allenhead bolts and remove the front engine cover.

Fitting instruction: When installing, be sure that the ventilating hose is firstly installed into front engine cover.

■

Remove hex.head bolt (arrow) with a socket wrench.

■

Remove starter by withdrawing it rearward.

12 41 170 Starter protection relay removal and installation

Remove fuel tank 16 11 030

Disconnect the negative cable at the battery, remove the two bolts and lock washers, unplug the five wire plugs.

Wire sequence
plug '87' = black wire
plug '15' = green wire
plug '30' = 3 red wires
plug '31b' = brown/black wire
plug 'D+' = 2 blue wires

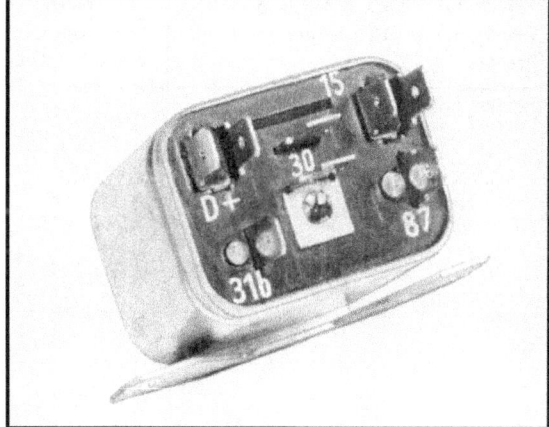

Starting Motor Service Diagnosis

Condition	Possible Cause	Correction
Starter fails to operate when starter button is depressed.	Headlight turned on: a) Lights are dim. Weak battery or dead cell in the battery. b) Light is on, but dims upon actuation of starter. Dead battery. c) Light is on, but dims as soon as the starter button is depressed. Loose or corroded battery cable terminals. d) Light is normal. Bridge terminals 50 and 30 on the starter. Starter turns. Starter button defect or faulty wiring. e) Light is normal. Starter solenoid is actuated but starter does not turn. Use auxilliary cable to connect battery ponsitive to terminal 30 on the starter. Starter turns. Solenoid switch contact corroded.	a) Test for specific gravity. Recharge or replace battery as required. b) Charge battery. c) Clean the terminals, apply a light film of petrolatum to the terminals after tightening. d) Replace starter button, repair open circuit. e) Replace solenoid.
Starter does not turn while a cable is connected directly from battery positive to terminal No. 30.	a) Worn brushes. b) Brushes binding. c) Brush spring pressure insufficient.	a) Replace brushes. b) Loosen brushes. c) Replace brush springs.
Starter runs at high RPM but does not turn engine, or turns engine intermittently.	a) Defective starter pinion. b) Broken teeth on flywheel drive gear. c) Starter pinion does not engage.	a) Replace pinion. b) Replace flywheel. c) Repair starter.

13 Carburation

Specifications . . . . Page 3
13 72 000   Air filter insert removal and installation 5

Specifications

Carburetion

	R 50/5	R 60/5	R 75/5
Type	Two inclined Bing slide carburetors with needle jet and concentric float		Two inclined Bing equal pressure carburetors with needle jet, vacuum piston, butterfly and concentric float
Carburetor			
Type			
Left carburetor	1/26/113	1/26/111	64/32/4
Right carburetor	1/26/114	1/26/112	64/32/3
Throat diameter	26	26	32
Main jet	130	130	140
Needle jet	2,68	2,68	2,73
Slide needle Nr.	3	4	46—241
Slide Needle position	2	2	2
Cold start jet	—	—	0,6 ϕ
Cold start air jet	—	—	2,0 ϕ
Mixture bore in rotary valve	—	—	2,0 ϕ
Idle jet	35	35	45
Idle air jet	—	—	1 ϕ
Idle air mixture screw position (turn opened)	0,5	0,5÷1	—
Idle mixture screw position (turns opened)	—	—	1÷1,5
By-pass passage	0,8 ϕ	0,8 ϕ	0,7 ϕ (at a distance of 6,2 mm from center of axle)
Float needle	2,2 ϕ	2,2 ϕ	2,5 ϕ

8.69

Specifications

Carburetion

	R 50/5	R 60/5	R 75/5
Type			
Throttle slide	22÷570	20÷570	—
Float weight	10 (0.35 oz.)	10 (0.35 oz.)	10 (0.35 oz.)
Vacuum slide weight g	—	—	102 (3.75 oz.)
Idle passage bore	0,8 ⌀	0,8 ⌀	—
Diaphragm	—	—	65÷811
Air filter	One common 'Micro-Star' filter element		

Fuel system:

	R 50/5	R 60/5	R 75/5
Fuel recommendation	Regular	Premium	Premium
Minimum octane (ROZ)	92	99	99
Fuel tank capacity	6 gallon of which one gallon reserve		

16 Fuel tank and fuel lines

Specifications . . . . Page 3
16 11 030   Fuel tank removal and installation 5

Fuel tank and fuel lines

Specifications

Type	R 50/5	R 60/5	R 75/5
Fuel tank capacity Ltr.		24 (6 gallons)	
Reserve Ltr.		3,5 (1 gallon)	

16 11 030 Fuel tank removal and installation

Disconnect negative cable from battery.
Remove steering damper rod, be sure to first remove circlip.

Close fuel pet cocks (1) remove fuel lines (2).

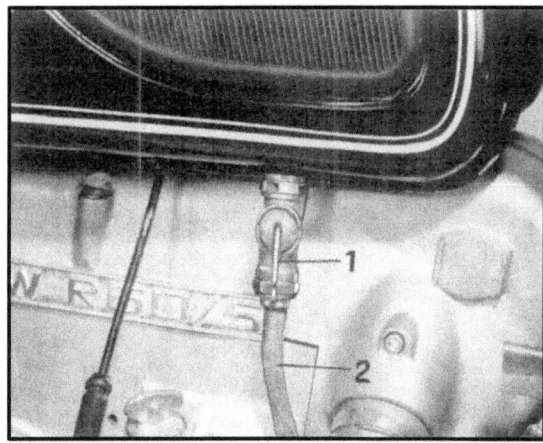

Flip up dual seat, remove wing nuts. Pull fuel tank to the rear then lift up at the front and remove.

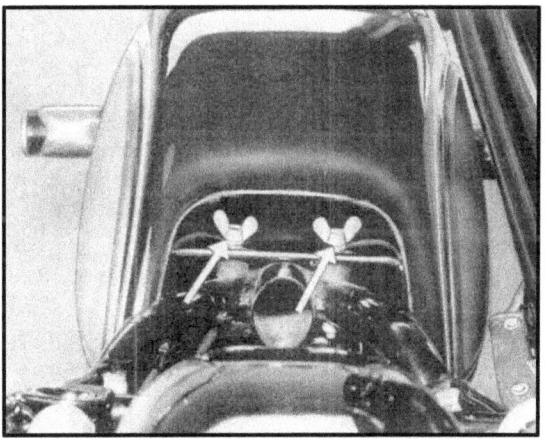

18 Exhaust system

Specifications . . . . Page 3
18 00 020   Exhaust system removal and installation 5
18 12 000   Muffler removal and installation 6

Specifications

Exhaust system

Type	R 50/5	R 60/5	R 75/5
Muffler diameter ⌀ mm		100 (3.94")	
Exhaust pipe diameter ⌀ mm		38×1 (1.496"×0.04")	

Torque specifications mkp (ft/lbs)

Finned exhaust pipe nut ft/lbs	20÷22 (144.7÷146)

All other screws and nuts should be tightened following the usual normal values quoted in the tables of the screw firms or in the new BMW standards sheet 60002.1.

18 00 020 Exhaust system removal and installation

Remove both exhaust pipe nuts, use wrench BMW No. 338/2.

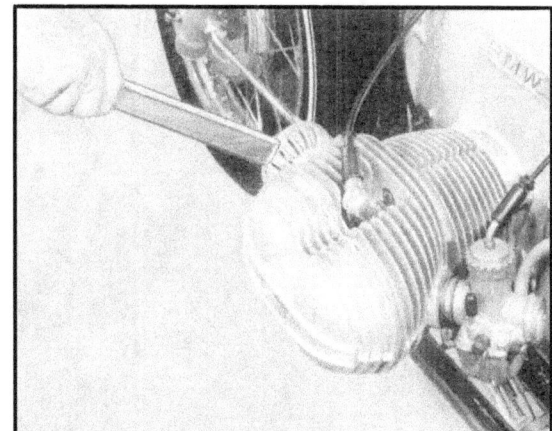

Remove the hex. nuts on the footrests and the hex. head-bolts on the frame.

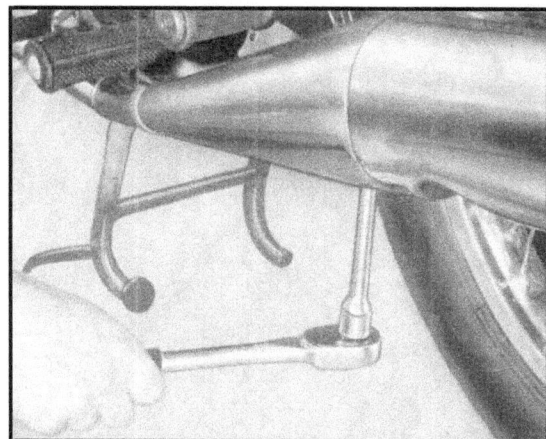

Loosen the allenhead bolts on the cross-over pipe and remove exhaust system.

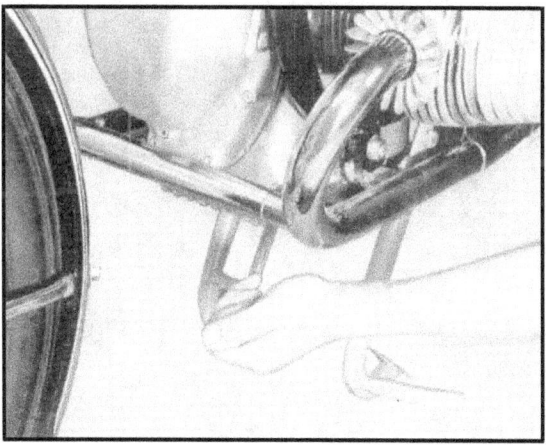

18 12 000 Muffler removal and installation

Loosen hex. head bolt of exhaust pipe clamp, slide clamp off muffler.

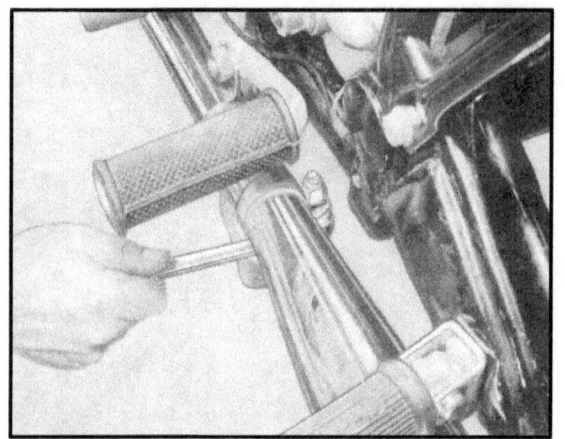

■

Remove hex. head bolt on the frame.

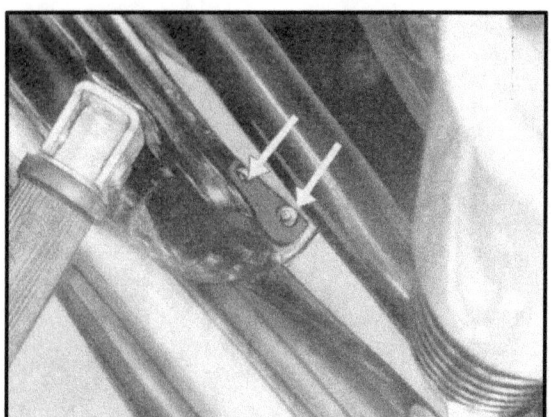

■

Pull muffler off to the rear.

■

21 Clutch

Specifications . . . . Page	3
21 21 500 Clutch removal and installation	5
21 51 000 Clutch lever removal and installation	7

Clutch

Specifications

Type	R 50/5	R 60/5	R 75/5
Type	Single plate dry clutch with diaphragm spring		
Marking (diaphragm spring)	"—"	"+"	without marking
Diaphragm spring pressure, installed kp	150÷165 (330.75÷363.83 lbs)	166÷180 (366.03÷396.9 lbs)	180÷220 (396.9÷485.1 lbs)
Height of diaphragm spring, free mm	17,5±0,5 (07"±0.02)		19,0±0,5 (0.75"±0.02)
Testing instruction or diaphragm spring	When placing the diaphragm border upon the measuring plate, the height difference of the spring tongues max. 0,3 mm (0.012") or when placing the spring tongues upon the measuring plate, the vertical runout of the diaphragm border max. 0,8 mm (0.032").		
Total thickness of the clutch plate (lamella and lining) mm		6±0,25 (0.24"±0.01")	
Min. thickness of the clutch plate mm		4,5 (0.18")	
Max. lateral runout of the clutch disc at the outer diameter mm		0,15 (0.006")	
Max. allowable runout of the clutch plate on outer diameter mm		0,3 (0.012")	
Max. runout of the diaphragm driving plate mm		0,1 (0.004")	
Max. allowable unbalance of the clutch plate cmg		6 (0.00834 oz)	
Clutch lever play (cable) mm		2 (0.08")	

Specifications

Clutch

Type	R 50/5	R 60/5	R 75/5

Torque specifications mkp (ft/lbs)

Lock nut for check lever adjusting screw	2,0÷2,3 (14.5÷16.6)
Clutch to flywheel	1,5÷2,0 (10.8÷14.5)

All other screws and nuts should be tightened following the usual normal values quoted in the tables of the screw firms or in the new BMW standards sheet 60002.1

21 21 500 Clutch removal and installation

First method
With engine removed; Engine removal according to
11 00 050
The pictures and text explain the procedure to be followed with the engine removed.

Second method
With transmission removed; Transmission removal according to 23 00 020
Engine remains in frame.

Loosen the 6 countersunk screws with an impact screw driver. Remove every alternate screw and install in their place a clutch clamp bolt, BMW tool No. 534. Tighten the clamp bolt and sleeved nut.

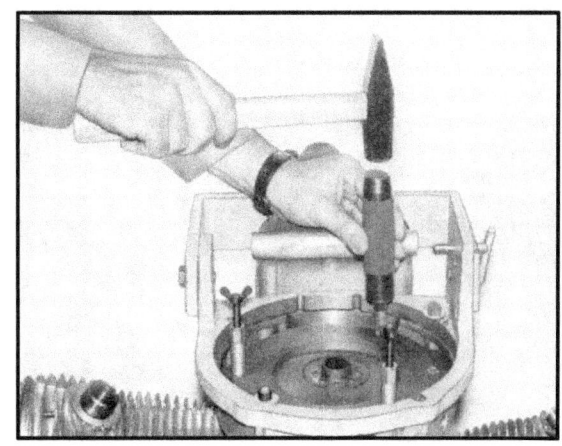

Remove the remaining three countersunk screws. Unscrew the three sleeved nuts of the clamp bolts evenly untill the diaphragm spring is fully relaxed.

Remove Clutch end-plate, six spacers, clutch plate, pressure plate and diaphragm spring.

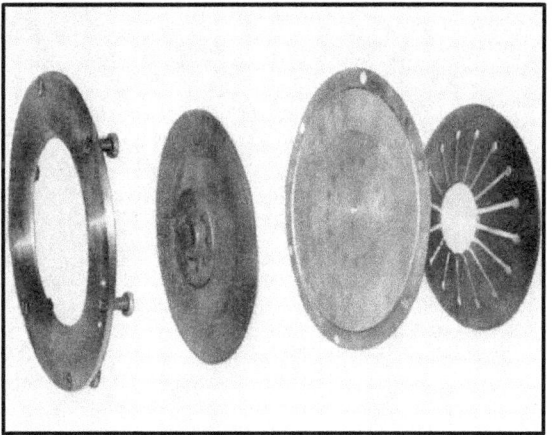

Inspection and repair:

Check clutch plate for wear and warpage, check diaphragm spring for required tension while installed. Check runout of clutch plate. For data see specifications.

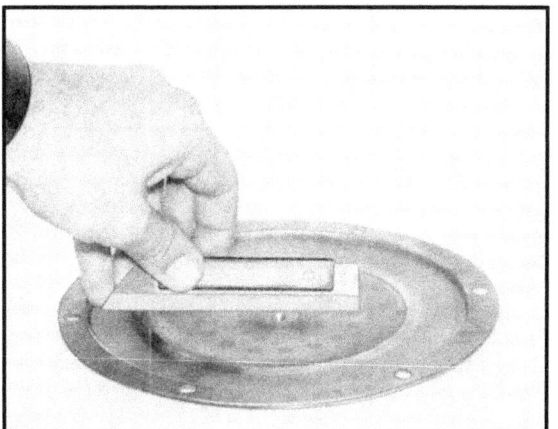

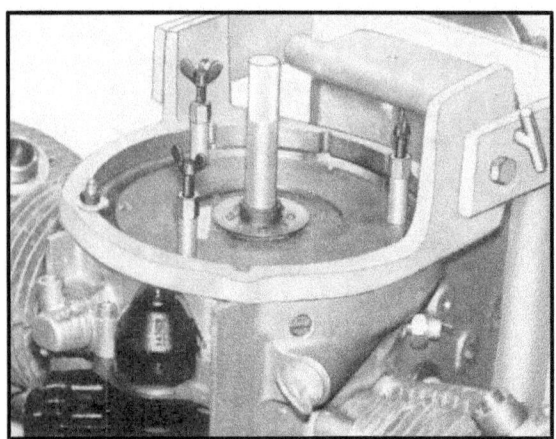

During reassembly use centering arbor, BMW tool No. 529, to properly position the clutch plate.

21 51 000 Clutch lever removal and installation

Unhook clutch cable (1).

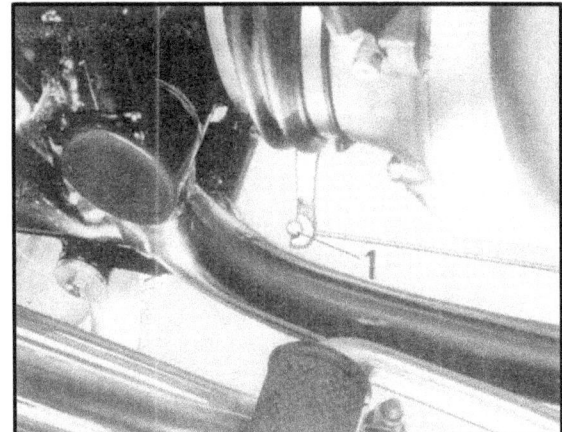

Remove cotter pin (2), withdraw pin (3) remove clutch lever and spring (4).

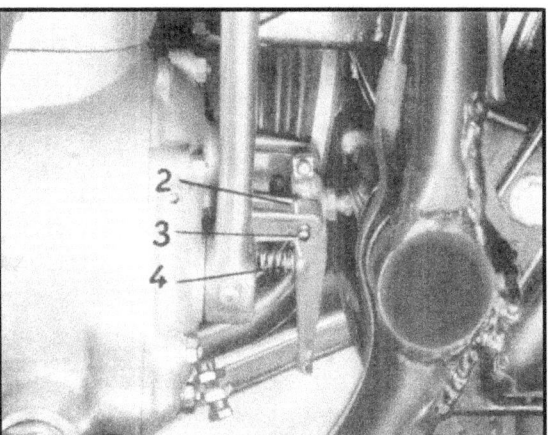

23 Transmission

Specifications	Page	3
23 00 020	Transmission removal and installation	5
23 12 531	Replacement of output flange and output flange seal	7
23 21 500	Input shaft and output shaft removal and installation	9
23 31 501	Shift fork replacement	13
23 31 851	Shift spring replacement	15
23 31 901	Neutral indicator replacement	17
23 51 501	Kick starter removal and replacement	18

Specifications

Transmission

Type	R 50/5	R 60/5	R 75/5
Transmission	Four speed transmission bolted to engine, shock absorber effective in all gears		
Type of shift	Ratchet type foot shift		
Gear ratios 1st speed 2nd speed 3rd speed 4th speed	3,896 : 1 2,578 : 1 1,875 : 1 1,50 : 1		
Oil recommendation	Name brand Hypoid gear oil SAE 90		
Oil capacity Ltr.	0,8 (0.845 US quarts/0.705 Imp quarts)		
Input shaft end play mm	0,1 (0.004") (adjusted with shims)		
Cluster gear end play mm	0,1 (0.004") (adjusted with shims)		
Output shaft end play mm	0,1 (0.004") (adjusted with shims)		
Ball bearing fit in transmission housing mm	Light preefit, for allembly heat the housing to 180—210°F		
Fit of gears on the bushings 1st & 4th speed play mm 2nd & 3rd speed play mm	0,040÷0,085 (0.0016"÷0.00328") 0,025÷0,075 (0.001"÷0.003")		

Specifications

Transmission

Type	R 50/5	R 60/5	R 75/5
Fit of bushings on output shaft			
1st speed play mm		0,005÷0,035 (0.0002"÷0.0014")	
4th speed play mm		0,005÷0,047 (0.0002"÷0.00188")	
Bushing for 2nd and 3rd speed has preefit on splines mm (Bushing can be replaced only together with shaft)		0,005÷0,047 (0.0002"÷0.00188")	
Output flange mm			
Radial runout mm		±0,05 (±0.002")	
Face runout mm		±0,05 (±0.002")	
Power transfer from transmission to rear wheel		Fully enclosed drive shaft in right swing arm tube, provided with a universal joint on the front and a semi-circular tooth coupling in the rear.	
End play of the foot shift lever mm		0,2 (0.008")	
Overshift play measured between shift pawl and shift cam plate in 1st and 4th gear mm		ca. 2 (0.08")	

Torque specification mkp (ft/lbs)

Bolts transmission to engine	2 ÷ 2,3 (14.5 ÷ 16.6)		Output flange to output shaft	22,0 ÷ 24,0 (159.1 ÷ 173.5)
Shift fork bolts	2,3 ÷ 2,5 (16.6 ÷ 18.1)		Transmission cover bolts	0,8 ÷ 0,9 (5.8 ÷ 6.5)
Stop ins for interlock pawl	1,7 ÷ 1,9 (12.3 ÷ 13.7)		Oil filler plug	2,8 ÷ 3,1 (20.2 ÷ 23.1)
Nut for kickstarter crank	2,0 ÷ 2,3 (14.5 ÷ 16.6)		Oil drain plug	2,3 ÷ 2,6 (16.6 ÷ 18.8)

All other screws and nuts should be tightened following the usual normal values quoted in the tables of the screw firms or in the new BMW standards sheet 60002.1

23 00 020 Transmission removal and installation

Put motorcycle on the center stand in addition prop the motorcycle up right behind the center stand.

Remove air filter 13 72 000

To remove right air filter housing, loosen nut (1) with a straight box-end wrench. Loosen hex. head bolt (2).

Remove right half of air filter housing. Pull breather hose off to the rear (3).

Loosen carburetor clamp and remove left carburetor.

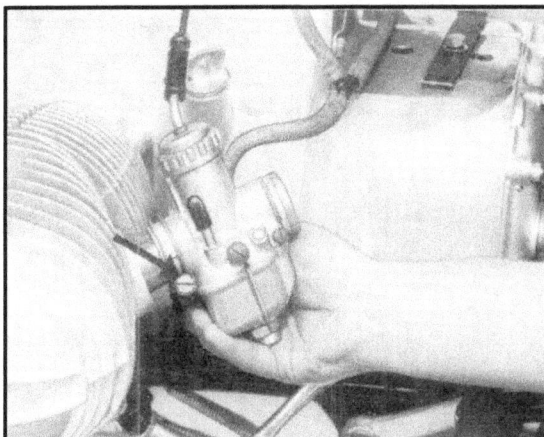

Pull up cable dust cover. Withdraw speedometer cable after removing negative cable and cable retaining bolt.

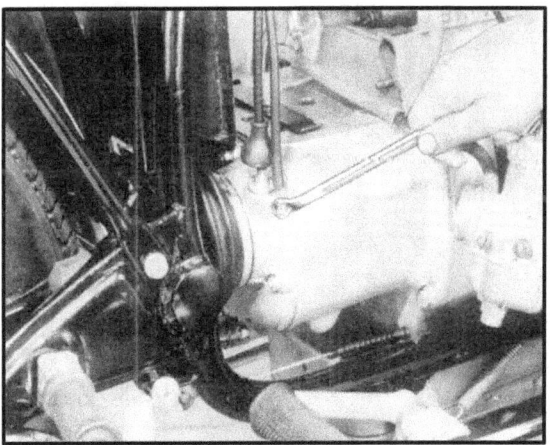

Remove drive shaft boot hose clamp and push boot back as far as possible.

Remove the four twelve pointed bolts and lock washers, depress foot brake to facilitate bolt removal.

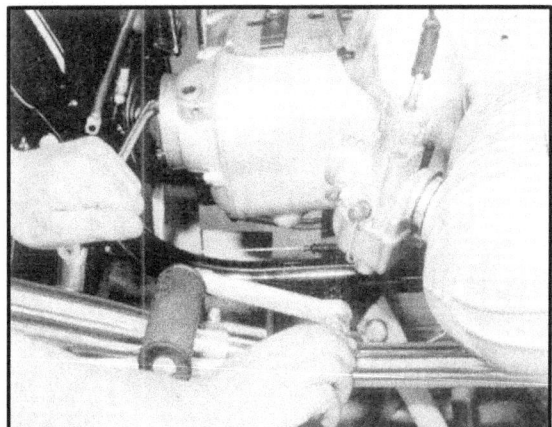

Remove swing arm bearing dust covers Loosen both lock nuts and remove both swing arm bearing pivot bolts. Observe torque requirements on reassembly (see 'Specifications').

■

Remove foot brake pivot bolt.

Remove Battery 61 21 010
Remove clutch lever 21 51 000

■

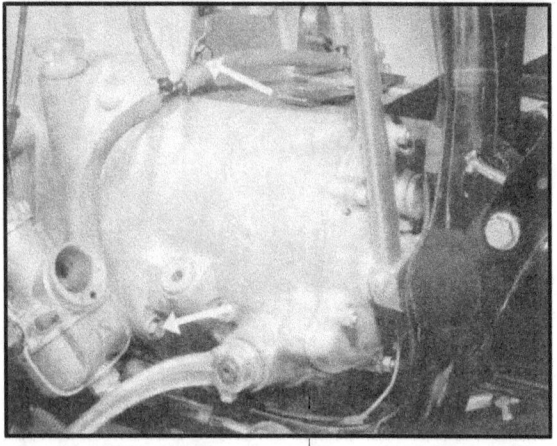

Unhook clutch cable on transmission. Remove the through mounting bolt bottom right, the longer bolt on top and the shorter bottom bolt.

■

Remove transmission partially to the left and disconnect the neutral indicator wire.

Remove the transmission.

■

23 12 531 Output flange seal replacement

Transmission removed according to 23 00 020

Install mounting fixture, BMW tool No. 6005/1 (for engine and transmission) into repair stand BMW tool No. 6000, vertically. Mount transmission in repair stand with two bolts M8×50.

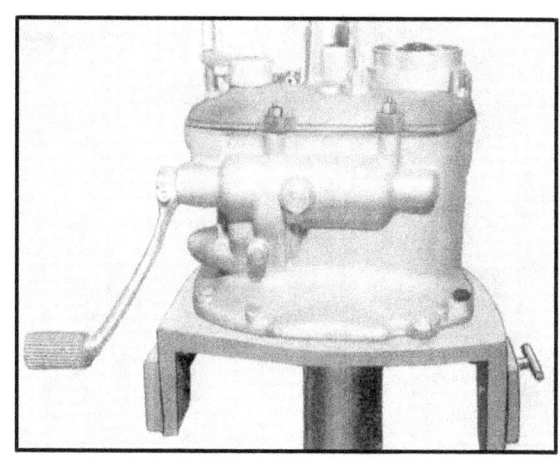

Remove speedometer cable hold down bolt and withdraw speedometer cable bushing with the help of two screw drivers. Remove speedometer drive gear.

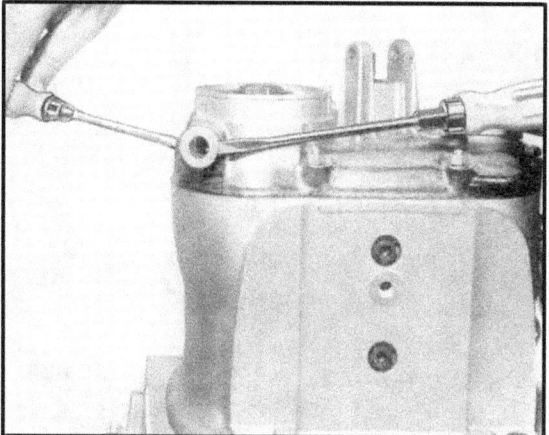

Bolt output flange holding fixture BMW tool No. 234 to output flange with four bolts M8 (hex.head size 13). Remove output flange nut (hex. head size 24 mm).

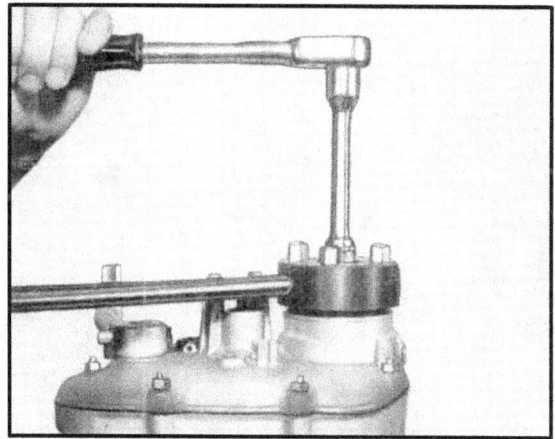

Install output flange puller BMW tool No. 232 with four bolts M8×1 (hex.head size 13 mm) and pull off output flange I necessary place a light hammer blow onto the puller spindle.

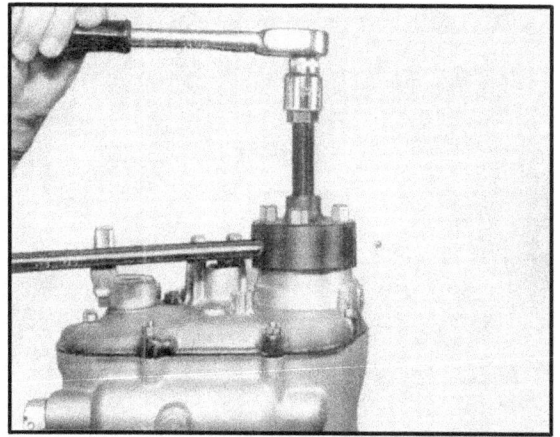

Remove clutch throw-out bearing and clutch push rod.

Remove the seven hex.nuts (hex.head size 10 mm) and the washers from the transmission cover.

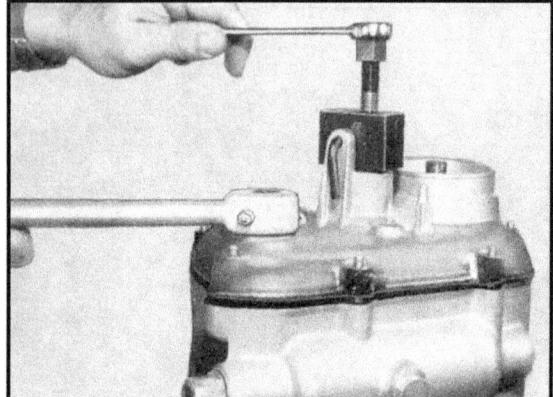

Heat transmission housing to 180—210° Fahrenheit. Install cover puller BMW tool No. 233 into clutch lever mounting bracket. Depress kick starter slightly and proceed to pull cover off. If necessary assist with a light mallet blow at the speedometer drive base.

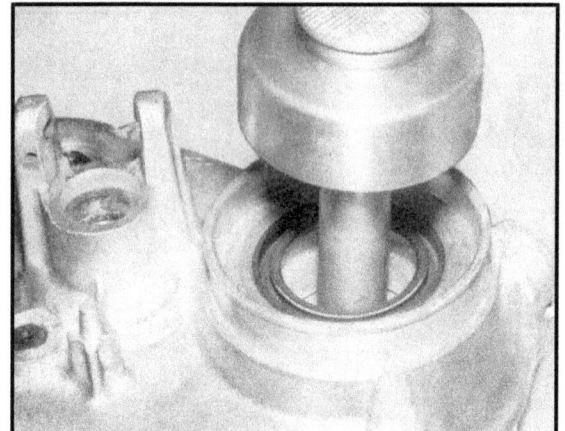

Remove spacer shims from cover. Remove defective output flange seal. Install new seal with drift BMW tool No. 231. Seal lip faces to the rear.

23 21 500 Output shaft and input shaft removal and installation

Transmission removed according to 23 00 020
Output flange seal replaced according to 23 12 531
Shift fork replaced according to 23 31 501

The preparatory steps explained heretofore should be performed only if necessary.

Remove input shaft from the still warm housing with a light mallet blow from the front.
Pull off thrust washer (11) and spring (10) together with kick starter gear (9).

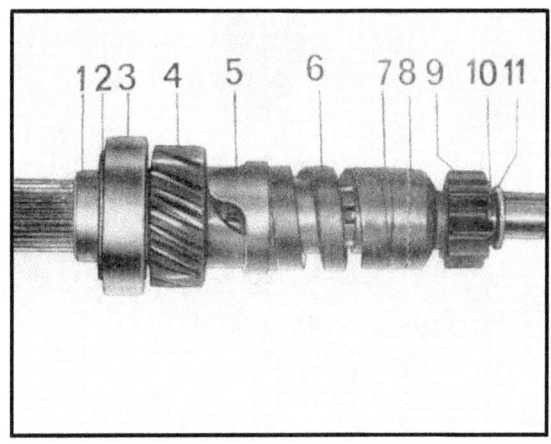

Compress shock absorber spring (1) using BMW tool No. 319/1 and remove circlip (8).

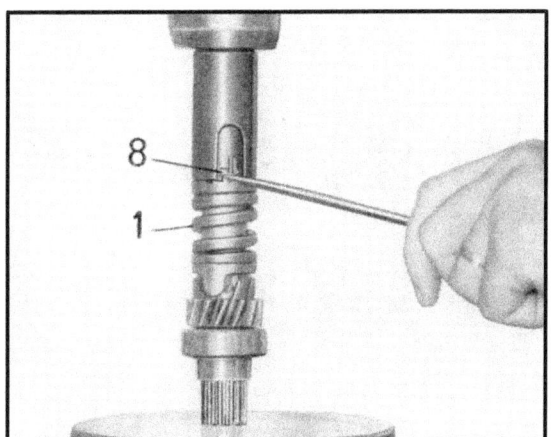

Remove kick starter ratchet (7) kick starter spring (6) drive coupling (5) and drive gear (4) from input shaft.
If necessary press off ball bearing (3) seal sleeve (1) and washer (2) for replacement.
When assembling the torsion damper, slide gear (4), drive coupling (5), damper spring (6), and kick starter ratchet (7) on the input shaft. Install circlip (8) using BMW tool No. 319/1 and 319/2, compress damper spring until circlip snaps into its groove.

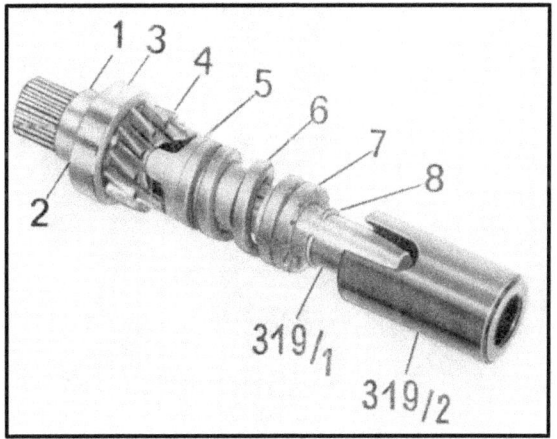

Slip on kick starter gear (9) and ratchet spring (10), now press on thrust washer (11). Always use a new thrust washer. The thrust washer has to be tight enough on the shaft so that it is not pushed off by the ratchet spring.

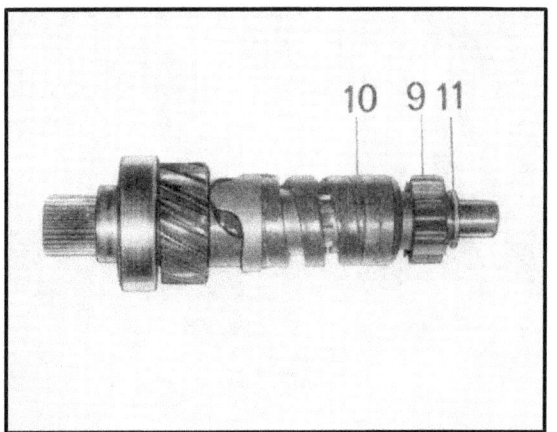

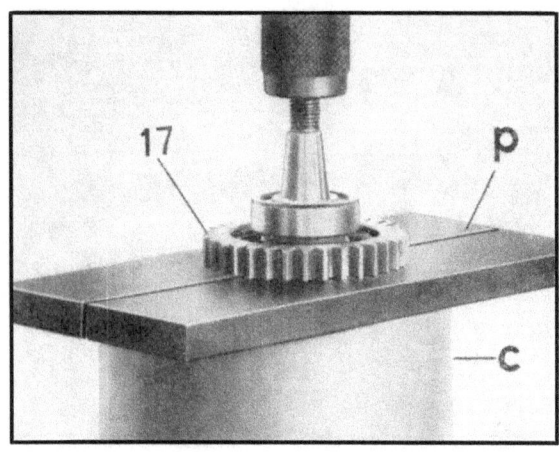

Place the divided plate p under the 1st speed gear (17), install the split plate upon an suitable press cylinder (c). Press off the speed gear together with thrust washer 19 and ball bearing 20.

∎

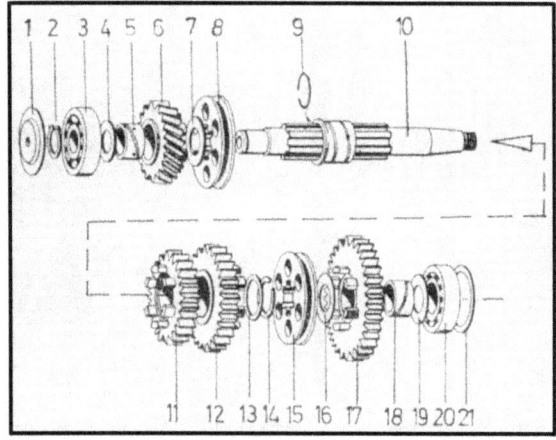

Remove floating bushing (18) of first gear, second washer (16) sliding coupling (15) for first and second gear.
Remove circlip (14) and splined washer (13), now remove second gear (12) and third gear (11).

∎

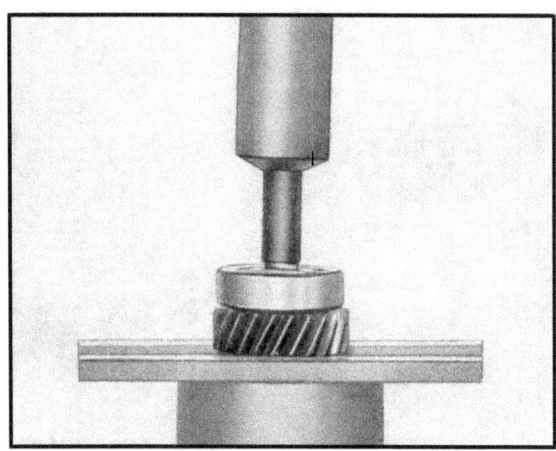

Remove circlip (2) from the forward end of the output shaft. Place two bars between fourth gear (6) and sliding coupling (8). Press off bearing (3) with appropiate mandrel.
Remove floating bushing (5), washer (4), washer (7) and sliding coupling (8). If the bushing for 2nd and 3rd gear is worn the shaft together with the bushing has to be replaced. Reassemble in reverse order.

∎

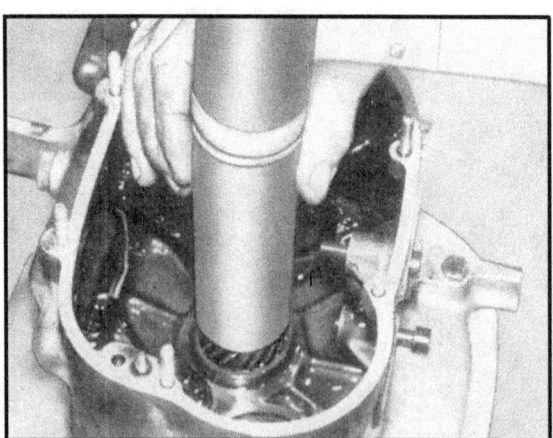

To install transmission shafts heat housing to 180—210° F. Place sleeve, BMW tool No. 206, on input shaft and insert input shaft into transmission housing. Under no circumstances should a hammer blow be directed against the end of the shaft. This would result in an improper fit.

∎

Before installing output shaft, lay oil guide into bearing bore.
Insert output shaft and cluster gear together with shift forks into the transmission housing. Be careful to prevent shift forks from binding. If the output shaft, sliding couplings, or shift forks were replaced, the shift forks have to be readjusted according to 23 31 501.

To measure the end play of the transmission shafts, install new gasket on transmission housing. Support output shaft with (fixture) BMW tool No. 504.
Measure distance from ball bearing to mating surface of housing.

Measure the distance from housing cover mating surface to bottom of ball bearing seat in cover. Shim out the difference allowing for 0,1 mm (0.004") end play. The cluster gear is measured out exactly the same way, end play 0,1 mm (0.004"). During installation of the cover the shims can be held in the cover with a small amount of grease.

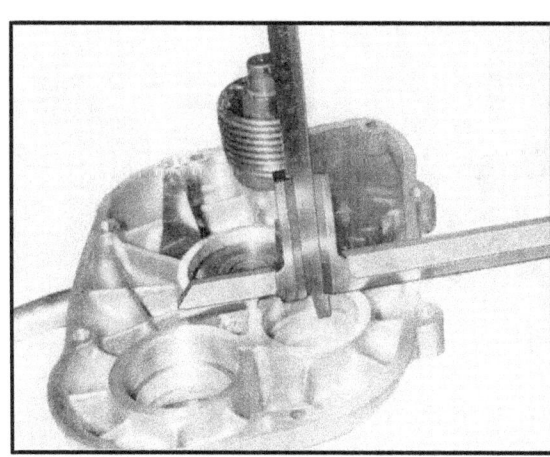

To facilitate measuring of the input shaft a 20 mm (0.8") bushing BMW tool No. 5061 is placed on the end of the shaft. Measure from the top of this bushing to the mating surface of the transmission housing. Subtract 20 mm (0.8") from the measurement. (This is the thickness of the bushing 5061).

8. 69

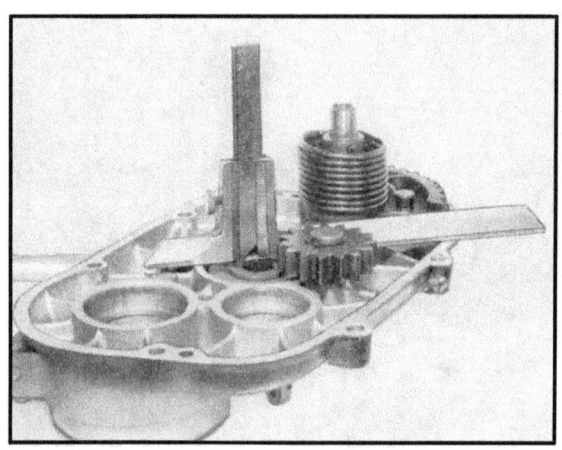

Measure from the mating surface of the transmission cover to the shoulder of the bushing installed in the bearing. The result has to be subtracted from the measurement obtained at the housing. allowing for 0,1 mm (0.004") end play. The remainder has to be made up by spacers.
b — (a — 20) — 0,1 mm (b — [a — 0.8"] — 0.004") = thickness of spacers required.

■

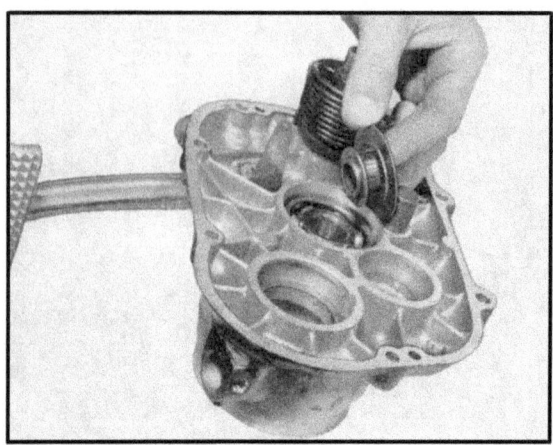

Remove bushing with shoulder from bearing. The determined cup shaped spacer (s) has to be placed on the bearing with the raised outer edge facing into the transmission. Reinstall bushing. The shoulder of the bushing must be included when measuring. We did so by installing it into the bearing before measuring.

■

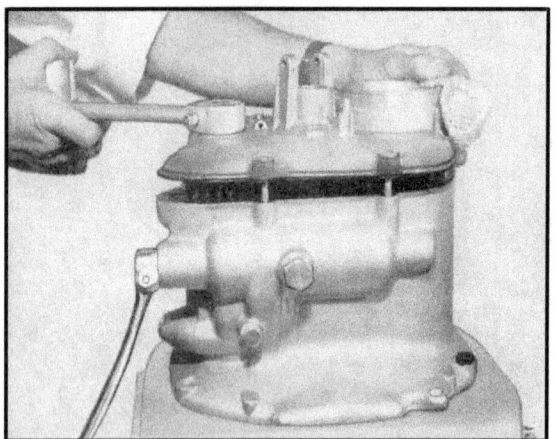

To install cover, heat it to 180 to 210° F. Place it on the transmission and depress kick starter partially. Move the kick starter up and down slightly to engage kick starter gear.

■

23 31 501   Shift fork replacement

Transmission removed according to 23 00 020
Output flange seal replaced according to 23 12 531

The preparatory steps explained heretofore should be performed only if necessary.

1) Mark mating shift forks and eccentric bushings. Remove the two allenhead bolts (hex.size 6 mm) and remove the washers and retaining plate.

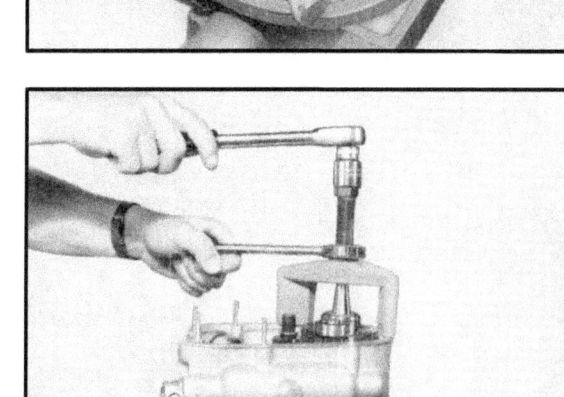

2) Withdraw output shaft from warm transmission housing using puller BMW tool. No. 235. Make certain that shift forks do not hang up.

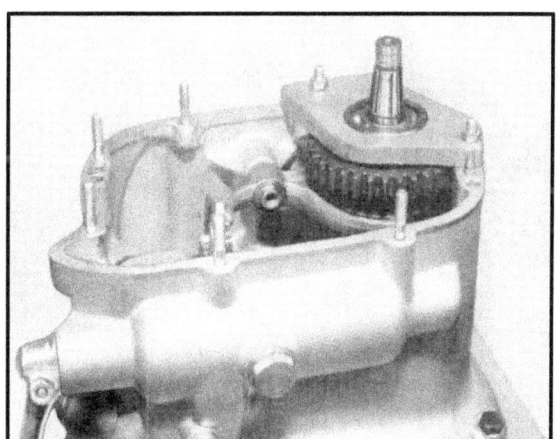

3) To adjust shift forks, heat transmission housing to 180—210° F. Install output shaft complete with sliding couplings and gears, and position it with fixture, BMW tool No. 504.

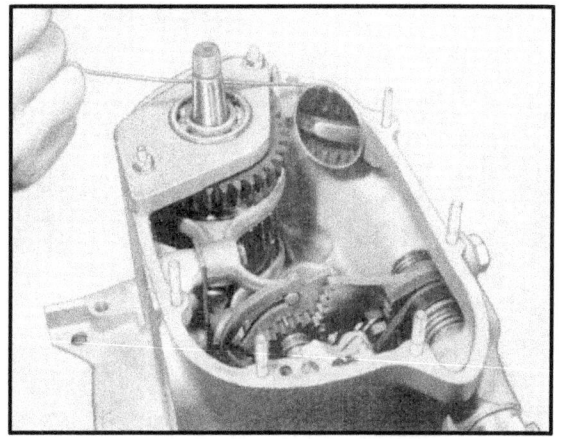

4) Install shift forks into sliding couplings and into shift cam plate and secure with allenhead bolts.
(the shift fork retaining bolts can be installed easily if the shift is placed into fourth gear for the installation of the bolt into the 3rd&4th gear shift fork, and into 2nd for the installation of the bolt 1st&2nd gear shift fork)

Shift into neutral, adjust the shift forks, at the eccentric bushings, with an open end wrench (hex.sizell) to bring the sliding couplings exactly into center between the gears. Verify this by checking with an inspection mirror.

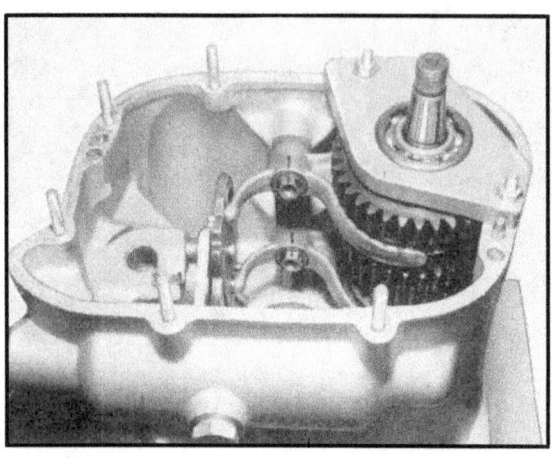

Check with inspection mirror and make certain that the the dowels are fully engaged into the sliding couplings, but that sliding couplings are not pressed against the gears.

■

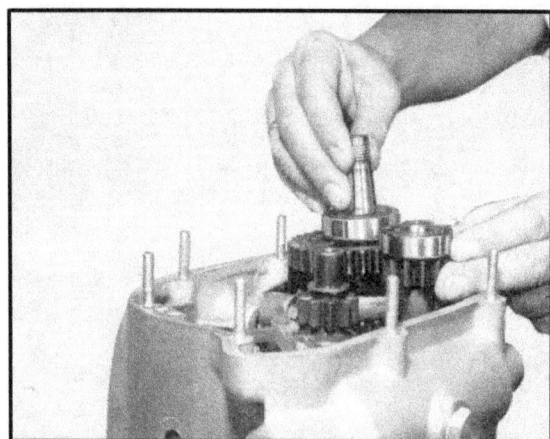

Mark the position of the eccentric bushing on each shift fork.

Remove output shaft from transmission housing.
Heat housing to 180—210° F. and install output shaft with shift forks and cluster gear. Make certain that shift forks do not hang up.

■

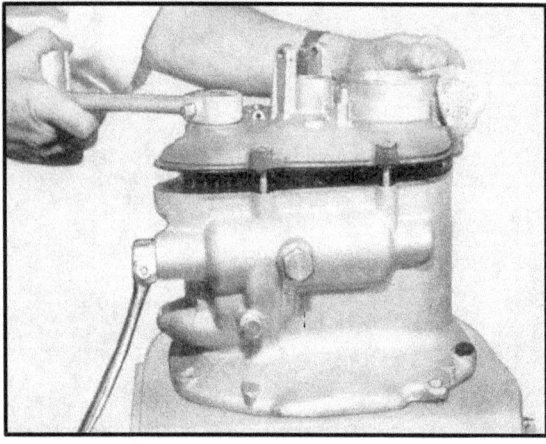

Heat transmission cover to 180—210° F. Place the shims for the shafts into the cover and install cover and output flange. For required torque see Specifications.

■

23 31 851 Shift spring replacement

Transmission removed according to 23 00 020
Output flange replaced according to 23 12 531
Shift forks replaced according to 23 31 501
Output and input shafts replaced acc. to 23 21 500
The preparatory steps explained heretofore should be performed only if necessary.

1) Remove circlip (1), remove shift cam plate. Remove circlip (2), remove washer and detent spring.

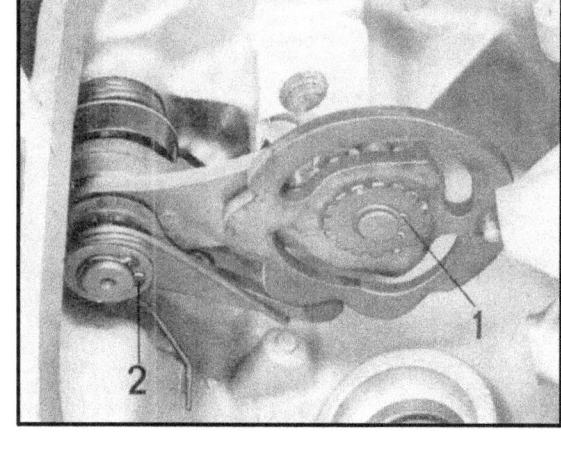

2) Remove circlip and remove pawl and shift segment.

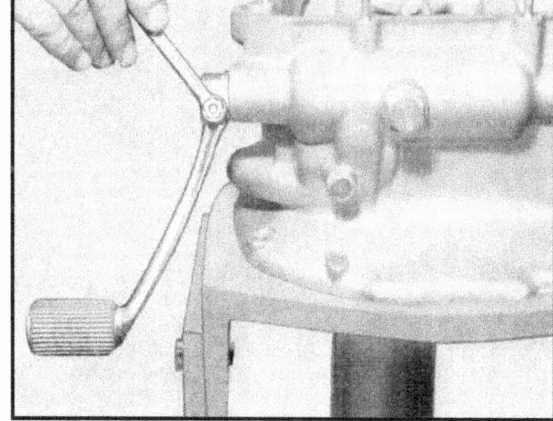

3) Remove nut (hex.size 10 mm) and drive out wedge bolt of shift lever.
   Remove shift lever and spacer.

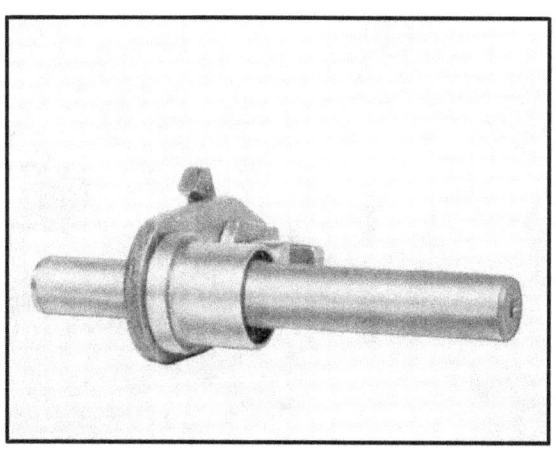

4) Remove shift selector assembly with bushing, holders, circular leaf spring, washer and return spring.
   Reassemble in the following order.
   1. Install bushing on shift selector assembly with the shoulder toward the inner lever.

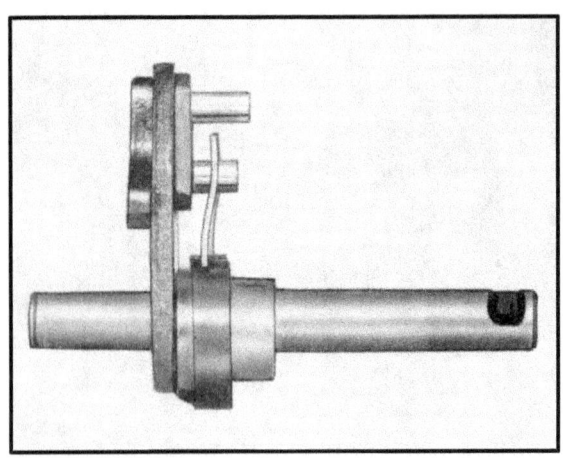

2) Insert the holders into the circular leaf spring and slide this assembly over the bushing, place the holders on each side of the short pin. Be sure that the crank of the levers is to the right (toward the selector).

■

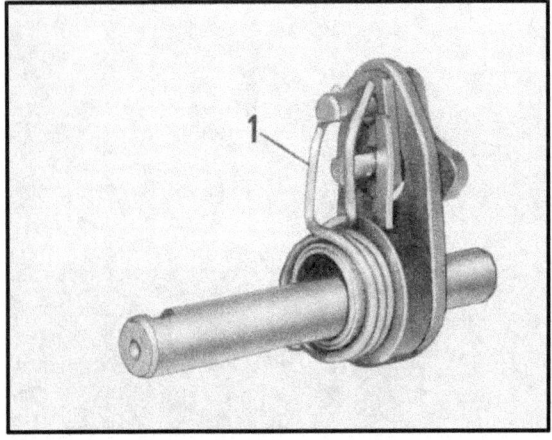

3) Insert washer.

4) Install the return spring with the curved end toward the inner lever. Insert the complete assembly into the housing, the return spring ends will fit over the pilot pin in the housing.

■

Install the foot shift lever, select the proper shims for the correct end play. Check Specifications.

■

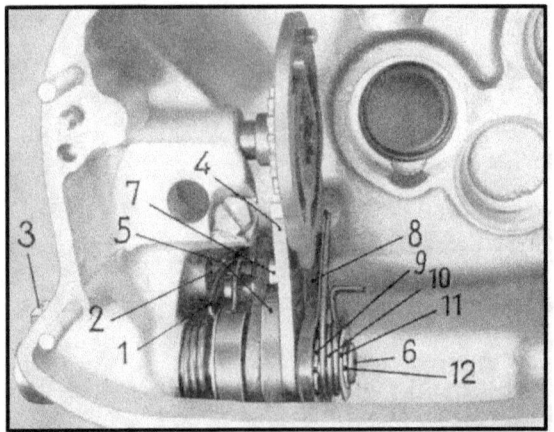

Slide segment (4) with selecting gear (5) on selector shaft (6). The selector lever engagement notches (7) have to have equal distance from the selecting teeth on both sides. If necessary correct deviation by bending the return spring. Install pawl (8) on segment (4) install circlip (9). Secure segment with circlip (12) after installing detent spring (10) and washer (11).

■

Insert shift cam plate, the second tooth of the segment (as viewed from the rear) has to mesh with the marked tooth of the shift cam plate.

The over-shift ([a] between pawl and detent notches) is determined by the selector gear limiting bolts. The over-shift should be 1 mm (0.04") in 4th gear on the upshift and on 1st gear on the downshift. If necessary correct this by shimming the limiting bolts.

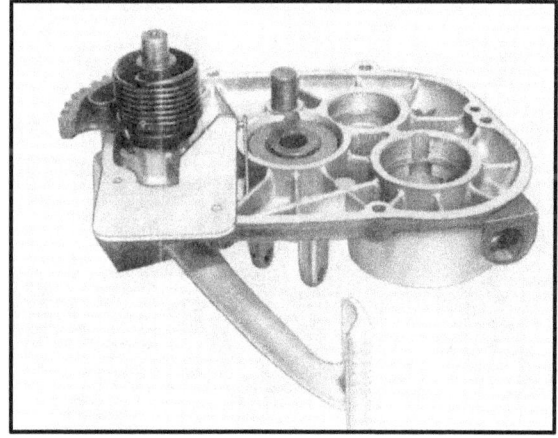

23 31 901   Neutral indicator replacement

Transmission renoved according to 23 00 020
Output flange replaced according to 23 12 531

The preparatory steps explained heretofore should be performed only if necessary.

After removing hex.nut (hex.size 10 mm) the contact spring, star washer, and flat washer can be removed. If necessary remove the insulating washer. The contact shaft and insulating bushing are installed with gasket cement. Check and adjust the position of the contact spring using gauge, BMW tool No. 5097.

After installing the cover check for proper operation with a continuity light. Withe the negative wire from the battery connected to the housing and the positive terminal light, the light should be lit in neutral and go off when connected to the neutral contact through a continuity shifted to 1st or 2nd.

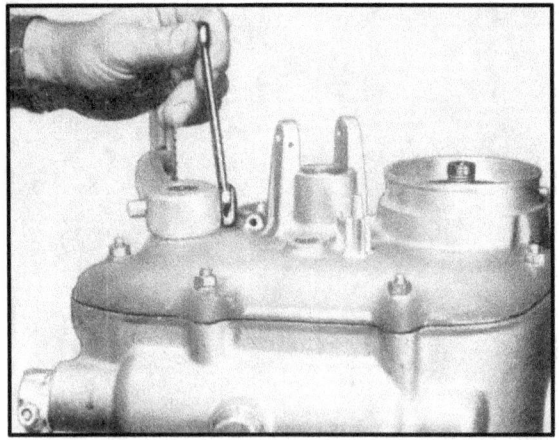

23 51 501 Kick starter removal and replacement

Transmission removed according to 23 00 020
Output flange replaced according to 23 12 531.

The preparatory steps explained heretofore should be performed only if necessary.

Remove hex.nut from wedge bolt, remove kick starter lever after driving out wedge-bolt. Remove kick starter quadrant with return spring from cover. Remove circlip from kick starter idler gear shaft and remove kick starter idler gear.

■

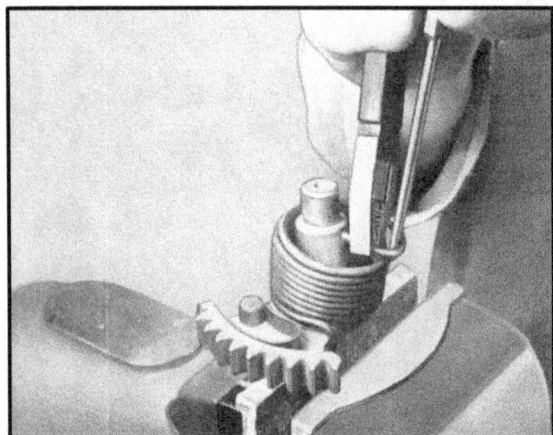

Caution: If the spring has to be replaced on the quadrant proceed as follows. Place the cranked end over the gear, wind the spring with the help of a screwdriver and insert the inward bent end into the hole provided in the quadrant. Assist with a pair of pliers.

■

When reinstalling the starter quadrant into the cover, insert the cranked end of the spring, into the hole provided in the cover, with a pair of pliers.

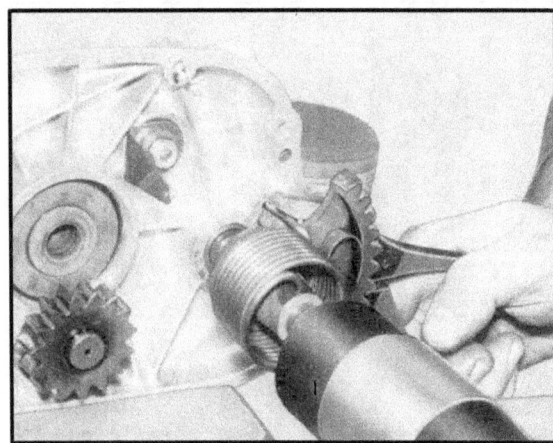

■

26 Drive shaft

Specifications . . . . Page 3
26 11 000   Drive shaft removal and installation 5

Specifications

Drive shaft

Type	R 50/5	R 60/5	R 75/5
Arrangement	Fully enclosed drive shaft in right rear swing arm tube, provided with a needle bearing universal joint in the front and a semi-circular tooth coupling in the rear.		
Oil recommendation	Brand name Hypoid lubricant SAE 90		
Capacity Ltr.	0,1 (0.105 US quarts / 0.088 Imp quarts)		

Torque specifications mkp (ft/lbs)

Coupling nut of internally splined bell-shaped gear	24÷26 (173.5÷188)
All other screws and nuts should be tightened following the usual normal values quoted in the tables oft the screw firms or in the new BMW standards shee- 60002.1.	

26 11 000 Drive shaft removal and installation

Rear swing arm removed according to 33 17 350

Clamp swing arm into vise, be sure to use jaw protectors. Insert fixture, BMW tool No. 508, into drive shaft bell and remove nut with corresponding socket wrench.

Pull drive shaft bell off. Use puller, BMW tool No. 204/2. Place a mandrel between puller spindle and drive shaft.
If necessary direct a hammer blow against spindle to help remove coupling.
Withdraw drive shaft from swing arm.

Assembly instructions: Clean and degrease the taper of the drive shaft and coupling before reassembly. (do not use gasoline for degreasing).
For torque requirement see 'Specifications'.

31 Telescopic Front Fork

Specifications	Page	3
31 42 009 Telescopic fork inspection		5
31 42 050 Steering damper removal and installation		6
31 42 100 Telescopic fork removal and installation		6
31 42 103 Telescopic fork disassembly and reassembly		9

Specifications

Front fork

Type	R 50/5	R 60/5	R 75/5
Wheel bearing lubrication	Multi purpose grease 360° F drip point		
Front wheel caster mm	ca. 85 (3.35") (not adjustable)		
Turning angle of handle bar	approx. 40° to each side		
Turning angle of front fork	46°		
Suspension travel (165 lbs load) mm Bump travel mm rebound travel mm	214 (8.42") 139 (5.7") 75 (2.95")		
Fork tube installation (measure from the top of the fork tube to the top of the lower fork yoke) mm	160 (6.3")		
Fork tubes	hard chrome plated		
Fork legs	aluminum alloy casting		
Lower fork yoke	drop forged aluminum alloy		
Oil capacity per fork leg Ltr.	0.28 (0.296 US quarts / 0.093 Imp quarts)		
Oil brand	Shock absorber oil, Shell 4001, Shell Aero hydraulic 4		
Fork tube outer diameter mm (hard chrome plated)	$36{}^{-0.050}_{-0.075}$ (1.417″ ${}^{-0.002″}_{-0.003″}$)		
Maximum allowable fork tube runout mm	0,1 (0.004")		
Fork tube (inner diameter) mm	$36{}^{+0.025}_{0}$ (1.417″ ${}^{+0.001″}_{+0}$)		
Clearance of fork legs on fork tube mm	0,050 bis 0,1 (0.002″—0.004″)		

Front fork

Specifications

Type	R 50/5	R 60/5	R 75/5
Shock absorber piston outer diameter mm		27,7 ± 0,1 (1.09" ± 0.004")	
Fork tube inner diameter at shock end mm		28 ± 0,15 (1.1" ± 0.006")	
Clearance of shock absorber piston in fork tube mm		0,05 ÷ 0,55 (0.002" ÷ 0.01375")	
Length of fork spring mm Centering nut		540 (22.1")	

Torque Specifications mkp (ft/lbs)

Centering nut	12,0 ÷ 13 (86.8 ÷ 94)
Clamp bolt on clamp ring	1,0 ÷ 1,2 (7.2 ÷ 8.7)
Upper spring retainer	12,0 (86.8)
Clamp bolts on bottom fork yoke	3,3 ÷ 3,5 (23.9 ÷ 25.3)
Shock absorber bolt bottom and shock absorber piston to shock absorber	2,5 ÷ 2,7 (18 ÷ 19.5)
Bottom cover on fork leg	12 ÷ 13 (86.8 ÷ 94)
Nut M 8 × 1 (holding shock absorber to fork leg)	2,3 ÷ 2,6 (16.6 ÷ 18.8)
Upper fender brace	2,3 (16.6)

All other screws and nuts should be tightened following the usual normal values quoted in the tables of the screw firms or in the new BMW standards sheet 60002.1.

31 42 009 Checking fork for damage

Front fork disassembled according to 31 42 103

If the fork was damaged, examine the upper and lower fork yokes as well as the fork tubes and fork legs thoroughly for hairline cracks.

Remove the fork tubes and check their runout between centers or on a truing stand, (max. allowable runout 0.1 mm [0.004"]).

Caution: Bent fork tubes can **not be straightened** (danger of fracture).

To check condition of lower fork yoke, install two new fork tubes (distance for checking, from fork tube to fork yoke 160 mm [6.3"]).

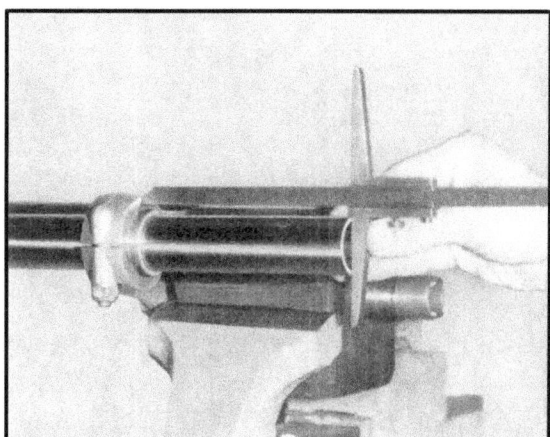

Place two straight edges, BMW tool No. 548, across the ends of the fork tubes. Align visually to determine any possible distortion.

Check that both tubes are parallel, with sliding calipers.

Check that steering head tube is aligned with fork tubes by mounting upper fork yoke. Both upper spring retainers and the centering nut have to screw on easily without binding.

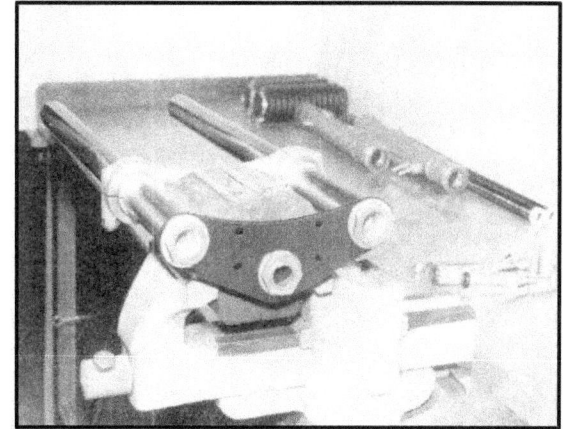

31 42 050 Steering damper removal and installation

Remove circlip and unscrew damper knob. Remove damper knob, spring washer and pressure plate. Remove the rubber guide ring inside the center tube.

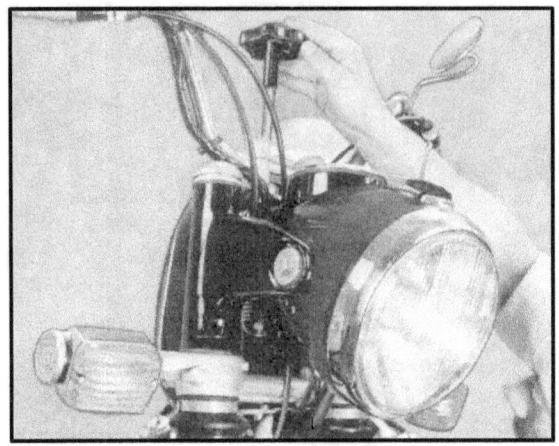

■

Remove allenhead bolt and lock washer from frame and remove damper plate.

■

31 42 100 Telescopic fork removal and installation

Remove front fender according to 46 61 000
Remove steering damper according to 31 42 050
Disconnect negative battery cable.
Remove upper and lower retaining screws from switch bracket.

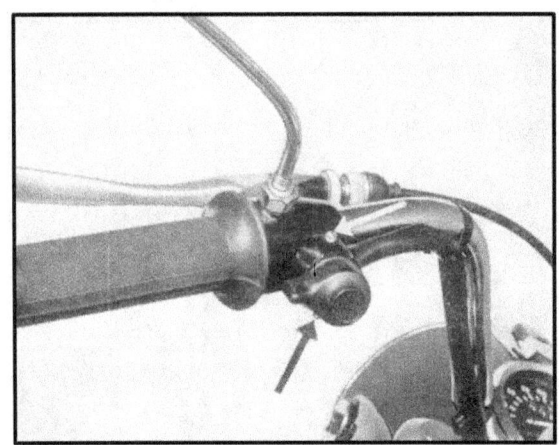

■

Remove cable straps from the handlebars, withdraw switch from switch bracket and remove switch bracket attachement screw (1).

Remove switch on the right side in the same manner.

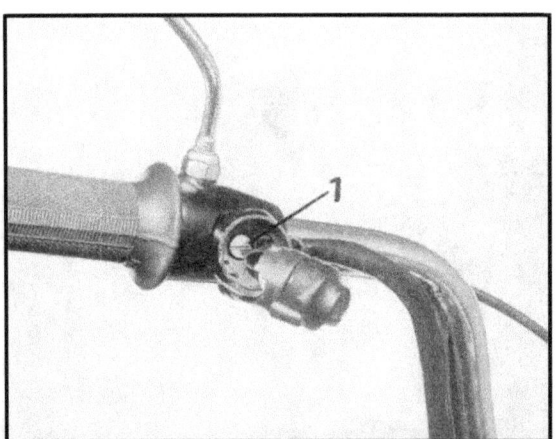

■

Disconnect negative cable at battery. Remove both headlight attachment bolts with rubber washers and rubber grommets. Suspend headlight carefully from the wiring harness.

Assembly instructions: Adjust headlight according to 63 10 004

Remove the handlebar brackets and lay handlebar on protected fuel tank.

Remove upper aluminum fork covers with a pin wrench. Remove both upper spring retainers (for torque see 'Specifications').

Special hint: During removal or installation place a spacer between the fork stops to protect fuel tank.

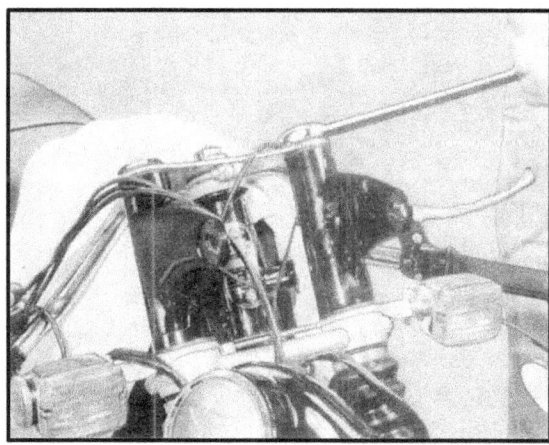

Remove centering nut and remove upper fork yoke. (for torque see 'Specifications').

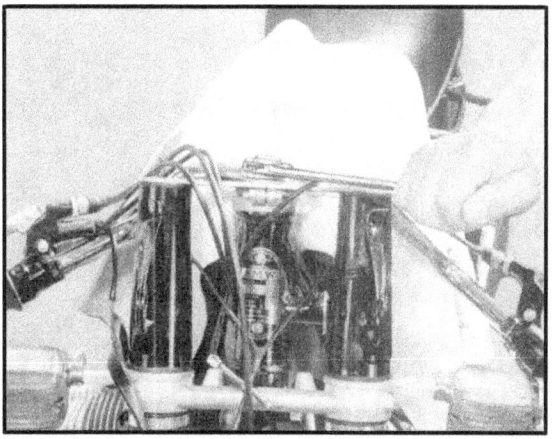

Assembly instructions: During reassembly route the cables correctly.

■

Remove turn signal lenses on both sides and disconnect the wires.

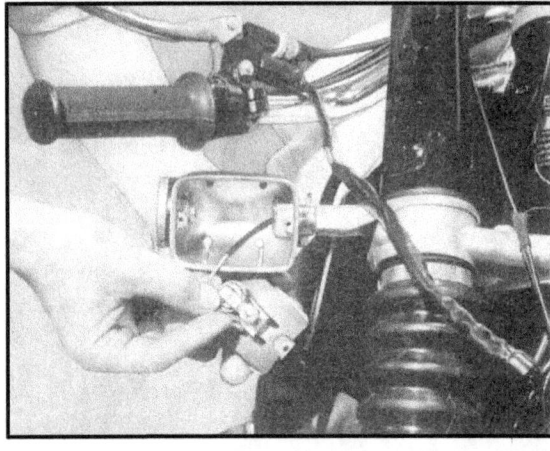

■

Remove headlight brackets with the rubber rings and withdraw the turn signal wires. (the lower fork yoke has vent passages and holes for the turn signal wires).

■

Remove allenhead clamp bolt and nut from the clamp ring and remove clamp ring (for torque see 'Specifications').

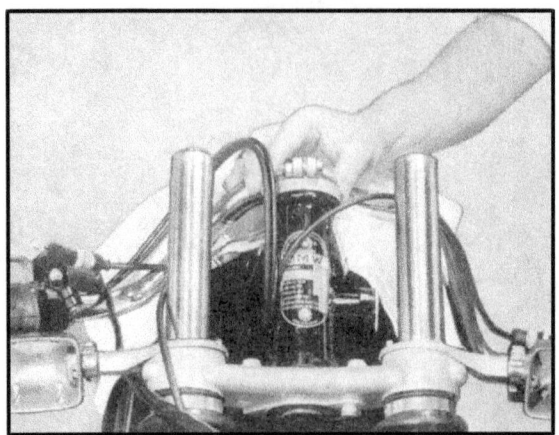

■

Remove turn signals with brackets.

Remove split ring nut. Remove dust cover.

Withdraw fork downward. If necessary tap the top of the steering head tube lightly with a mallet.

Protect tapered roller bearings. The outer races of the upper and lower bearings remain in the frame.

Assembly instructions: Before installations grease bearing races and tapered roller bearings.

Insert upper bearing (1). Insert fork carefully together with bottom bearing (2).

Caution: Watch the brand of the bearings, do not intermix races.

Install dust cover and install split ring nut. Tighten ring nut sufficiently to remove all play. Tap top of tube and bottom of the fork yoke to take up any slack. Install the clamp ring.

During tightening of the clamp ring the threads will engage somewhat further. This could cause the fork to get tight. If necessary loosen the ring nut 1/8 turn reinstall clamp ring.

The steering head bearings are correctly adjusted if the fork falls to either side (with the clamp ring fully tight) of its own weight and no play can be felt in the bearings.

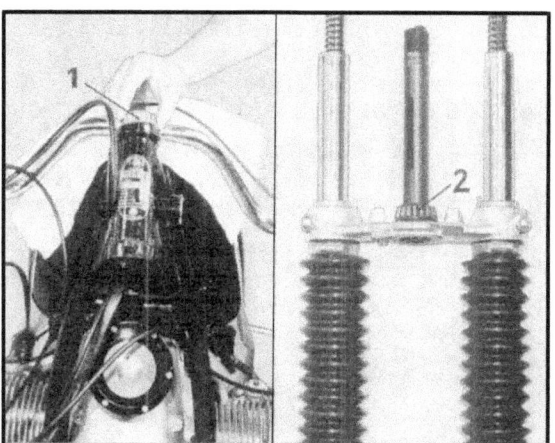

31 42 103 Telescopic fork diassembly and reassembly

Fork removed according to 31 42 100

Drain oil from fork.
Clamp fork into vise, use wood fixture BMW tool No. 545.

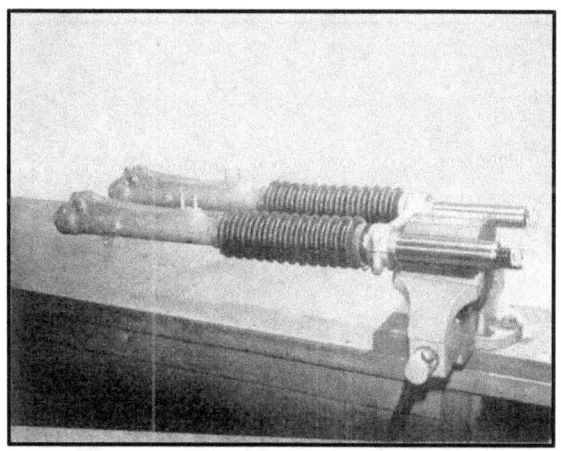

Loosen boot clamps. Remove bottom dust cover. Remove shock absorber retaining nut, hold shock absorber bottom bolt with allen wrench. (for torque see 'Specifications').

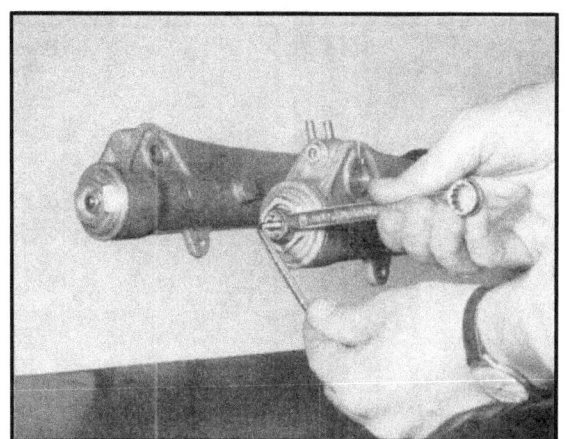

8.69

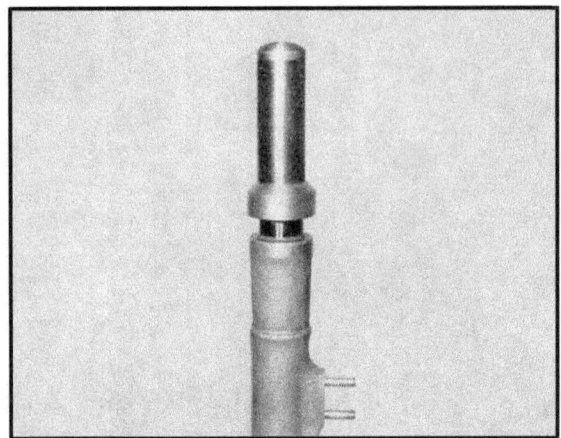

Withdraw fork legs.

Installation instruction: When installing new fork seals into the fork legs, coat the outer edge of the seal with gasket cement. Press seal into fork leg using mandrel, BMW tool No. 547. (the narrow seal lip and the metal edge face up) If KACO brand seals are used they should be installed without gasket cement and with the open end facing down.

■

Assembly instructions: When installing rubber fork boots slide vent hole over the vent tubes of the lower fork yoke.

■

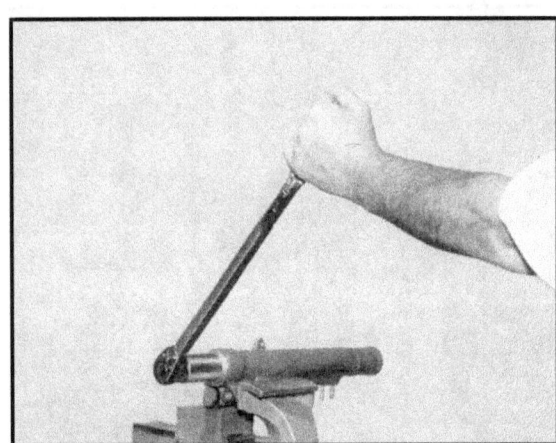

Remove bottom covers.

Assembly instructions: Torque bottom fork covers during reassembly (for torque see 'Specifications').

■

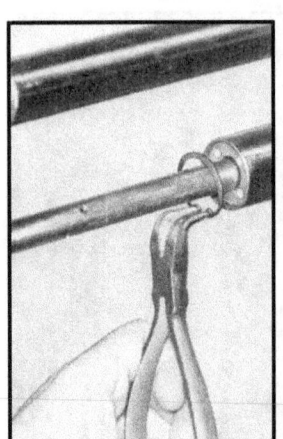

Remove gaskets from bottom shock bolts.

Assembly instructions: On reassembly always use new gaskets.

Remove circlip from bottom of fork tubes and remove oil orifice with a pin wrench.

■

Withdraw shock absorber, with the plastic bottoming ring and spring, **downward.**

Assembly instruction: To insert shock absorber into fork tube use ring compressor BMW tool No. 546 to compress scraper rings.

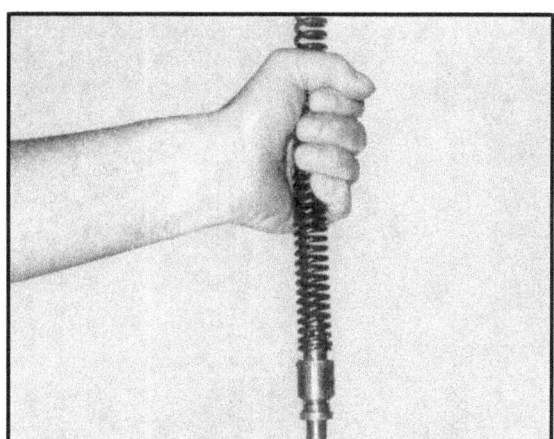

Remove springs from shock absorbers.
Remove or install springs on shock absorbers by turning them to the right.

Loosen clamp nuts on lower fork yoke (for torque see ('Specifications'). Insert spreading wedge BMW tool No. 549 and withdraw fork tubes.

Assembly instruction: If the lower fork yoke is replaced, install first the lower and upper fork yoke into the frame. Adjust the steering head bearings, after this is completed, the fork tubes should be pushed through the lower fork yoke and pushed up until they are flush against the upper fork yoke. Tighten clamp bolts allow the upper spring retainer to be tightened. (for torque see 'Specifications') If only one fork tube is replaced, the required height can be determined from the remaining fork tube.

Telescopic fork inspection 31 42 009

Clamp the hex of the bottom shock absorber retainer into the vise.
Unscrew the spring support with the piston rings. Remove the damper valve and spring. To remove opposite ball valve clamp shockabsorber tube into vise using jaw protectors. Unscrew retainer and remove spring and ball.

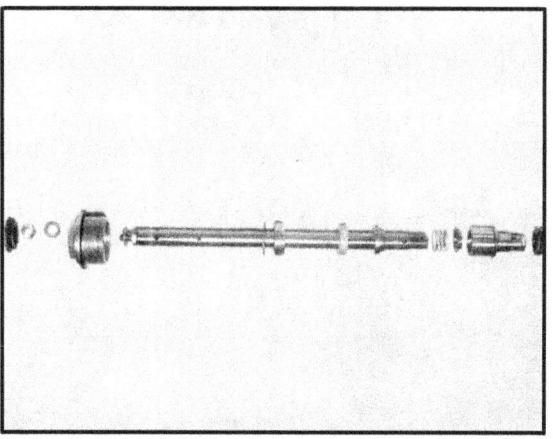

8. 69

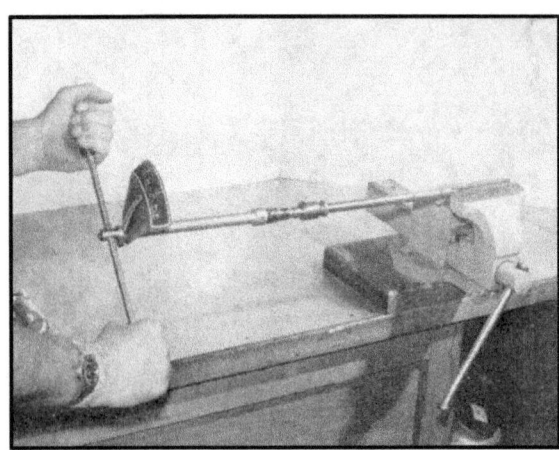

Assembly instructions: Reassemble shock absorber in reverse order. Clamp the hex. of the bottom retainer in vise and tighten both ends simultaneously by tightening at the hex. of the spring retainer. (for torque see 'Specifications').

Upon completion fill each fork leg with 280 cc of hydraulic oil (for type see 'Specifications'). Pump the fork 4 to 5 times to bleed it.

■

32 Steering and Handlebars

Specifications		Page 3
32 00 454	Adjusting the steering head	5
32 71 000	Handlebar removal and installation	6
32 73 030	Throttle cable removal and installation	7

Specifications

Steering

Type	R 50/5	R 60/5	R 75/5
Turning angle of handlebars		approx. 40° to each side	

Torque requirements mkp (ft/lbs)

allen head clamp bolt on clamp ring   1,0÷1,2 (7.23÷8.7)

Centering nut for telescopic fork   12,0 (86.8)

All other screws and nuts should be tightened following the usual normal values quoted in the tables of the screw firms or in the new BMW standards sheet 60002.1.

32 00 454 Steering head bearing adjustment

Remove circlip and unscrew damper knob. Remove damper knob, spring washer and pressure plate. Remove the rubber guide ring inside the center tube.

Disconnect negative battery cable.
Remove both headlight attachment bolts with rubber washers and rubber grommets. Suspend headlight carefully from the wiring harness.

Assembly instructions: Adjust headlight according to 63 10 004.

Remove handlebar brackets, protect fuel tank and lay handlebar carefully on tank.

Remove allenhead clamp bolt from clamp ring (2). Loosen centering nut (1). Insert drift through the slot in the clampring into the split ring nut, tighten sufficiently to remove all play of the bearings. Tap lower fork yoke and center tube with a mellet to insure seating of the bearings. Tighten clamp ring (2). The steering head bearings are correctly adjusted if the fork falls to either side (with the clamp ring fully tight) of its own weight and no play can be felt in the bearings.

Assembly instruction: For required torque see 'specifacations'.

32 71 000 Handlebar removal and installation

Disconnect negative battery cable.

Remove circlip and unscrew damper knob.
Remove damper knob, spring washer and pressure plate.
Remove the rubber guide ring inside the center tube.

■

Remove handlebar brackets, protect fuel tank and lay handlebar carefully on tank.

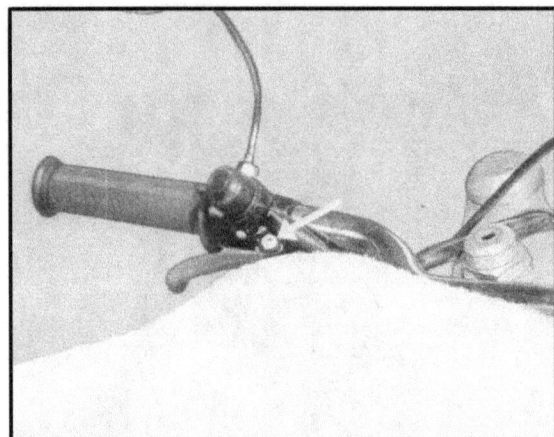

■

Remove left grip. Loosen allen head bolt (arrow) and remove clutch lever bracket. Watch out for wedge.

■

Loosen allen head bolt on throttle assembly and withdraw assembly from handlebar. Watch for wedge.

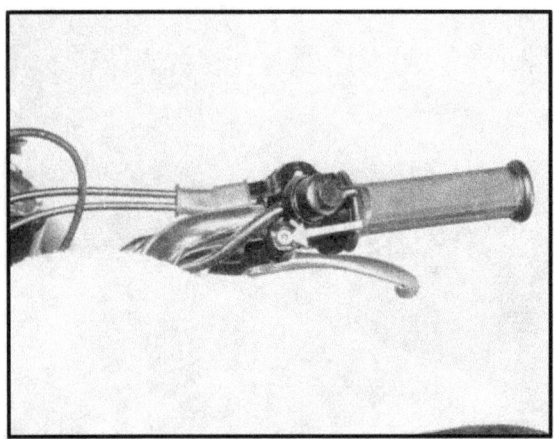

■

33 Rear drive

		Page
Specifications		3
33 10 010	Rear drive unit removal and installation	5
33 10 113	Rear drive unit disassembly and reassembly	6
33 12 051	Ring and pinion gear replacement	10
33 12 054	Ring gear backlash and endplay adjustment	11
33 17 350	Swing arm removal and installation	13
33 17 363	Swing arm disassembly	14
33 52 000	Shock absorber removal and installation	14
33 52 053	Shock absorber disassembly and reassembly	14

33 10 010 Rear drive unit removal and installation

Remove rear wheel according to 36 30 320
Support swing arm under pivot bolts in the front. Remove nut from spring unit.

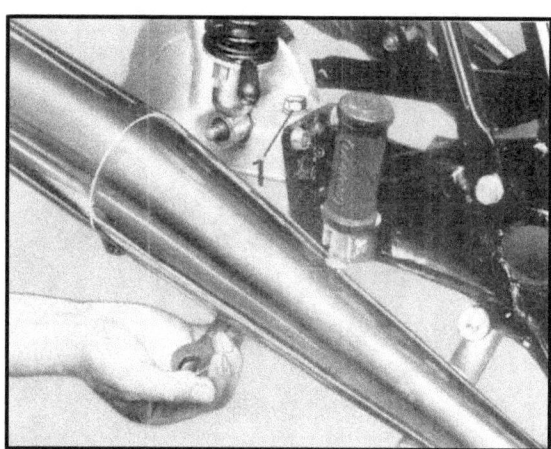

Drain oil from right swing arm tube. To facilitate draining remove filler plug also.

Assembly instruction: After reinstallation fill swing arm tube with 0.1 ltr. oil (for type of oil see 'Specifications').

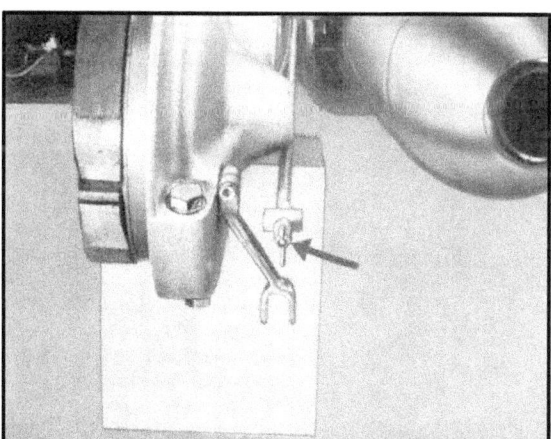

Remove wing nut from brake rod. Withdraw transverse pin from brake lever reinstall it on the brake rod and reinstall wing nut.

Loosen upper shock unit mounting bolt, remove the four nuts that hold rear drive to swing arm.

Withdraw rear drive from swing arm.

Assembly instruction: To facilitate installation, put transmission in gear and turn drive shaft by depressing kick starter until teeth of coupling mesh.

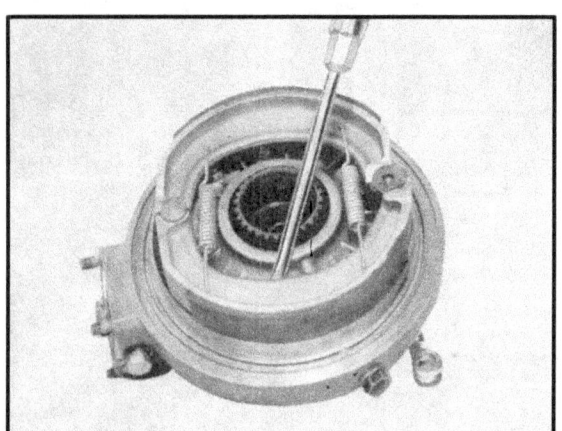

33 10 113 Rear drive unit disassembly and reassembly

Remove rear drive unit according to 33 10 010
Drain oil.

Assembly instruction: After reinstallation fill rear drive with 0.25 ltr. oil (for type see 'Specifications').

Remove the brake shoes by lifting the shoe on the flattened side of the washer off its position first.

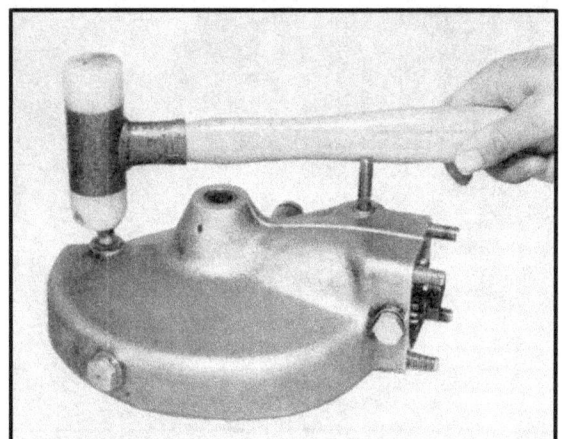

Remove nut from brake cam. Remove brake lever by tapping brake cam with a mallet inward.

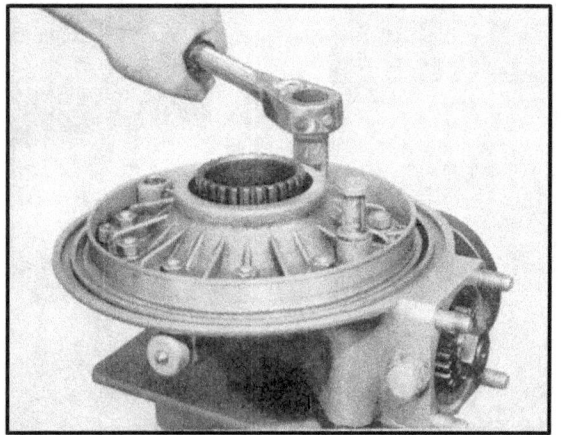

Using tool BMW No. 261, clamp rear drive unit into Workstand BMW No. 6000.
Remove the 10 nuts and washers from the housing cover.

To protect seal install seal sleeve BMW tool No. 505 (1) over splines.

Cover can be pulled off with two bolts (2), that are screwed into the two threaded holes of the cover. This will remove the cover, ball bearing, ring gear, and needle bearing inner race.

Caution: Remove the brass spacer, keep for re-use.

Assembly instruction: To reinstall cover heat it to 180° F.

Remove large seal from cover.

Assembly instruction: Install new seal using drift BMW tool No. 251 and handle BMW tool No. 5120.

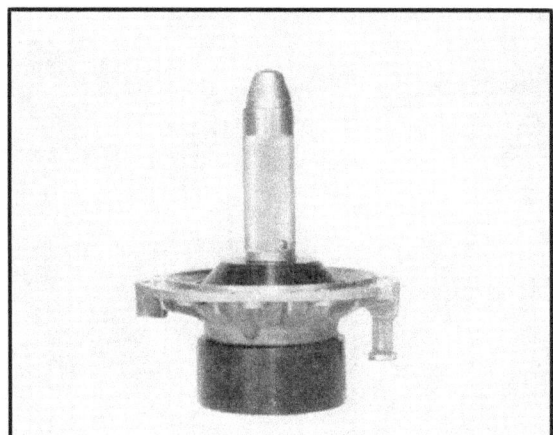

Heat housing to 180° F and remove needle bearing.

Assembly instruction: Install needle bearing with drift BMW tool No. 257 and handle BMW tool No. 5120.

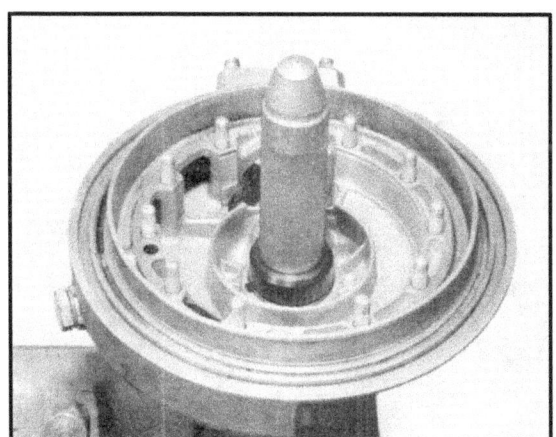

Pull needle bearing race from ring gear.

Assembly instruction: Install race using drift BMW tool No. 254.

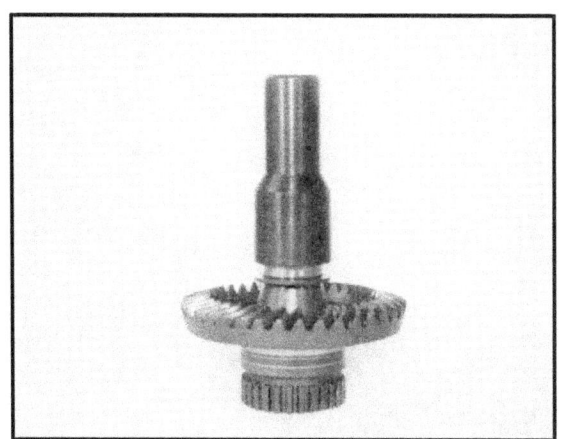

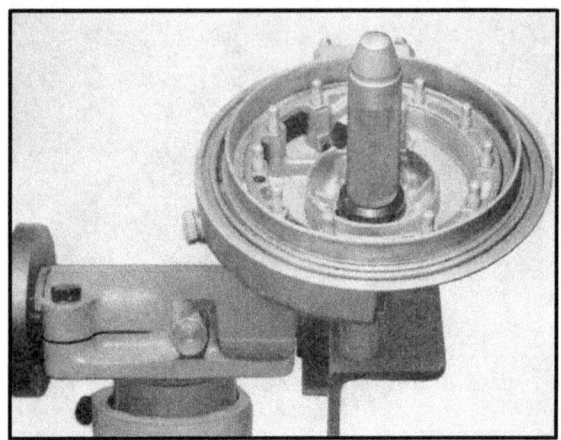

Remove seal from housing.

Assembly instruction: Install seal with drift, BMW tool No. 258, and handle BMW tool No. 5120.

■

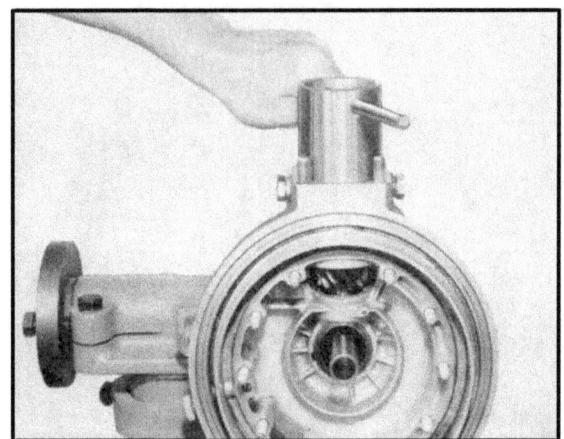

Remove lock tab, install holder BMW tool No. 256 and remove pinion nut. Withdraw drive pinion.

Caution: Always replace lock tab of pinion nut. (For torque see 'Specifications'.)

■

Remove threaded ring including seal with pin wrench, BMW tool No. 253. Remove inner spacer washer.

Assembly instruction: Install inside spacer washer and lock tab with gasket cement.

■

Remove seal from threaded ring.

Assembly instruction: Install new seal using drift BMW tool. No. 255 and handle BMW tool No. 5120.

■

Withdraw pinion together with double-row ball bearing. Use puller, BMW tool No. 259 with fixture, BMW tool No. 259/1.

To replace pinion needle bearing, remove recessed pin, heat housing to 180° F. and remove bearing.

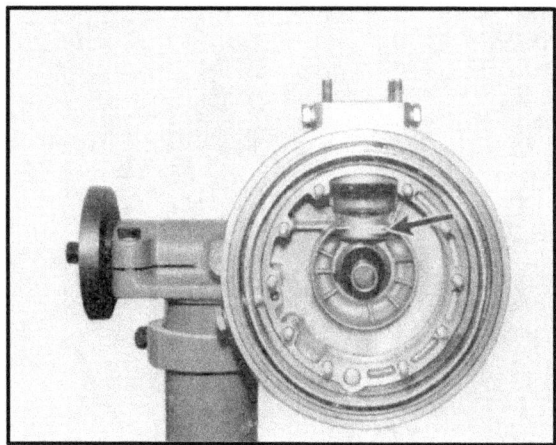

Assembly instruction: Install pinon needle bearing with drift, BMW tool No. 252.

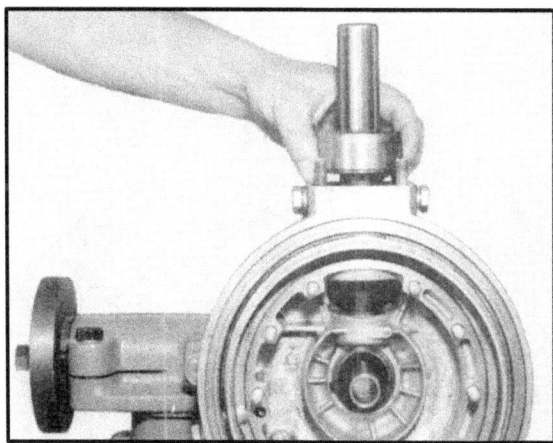

Tap off large ring gear ball bearing through the holes in the ring gear using a soft metal drift.

Assembly instruction: Heat ball bearing to approximately 180° F for installation.

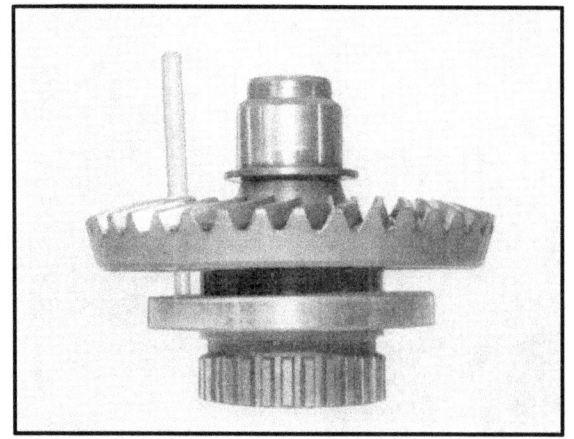

33 12 051 Ring and pinion gear replacement

Rear drive unit disassembly according to 33 10 113
Ring and pinion gears are matched and replacable only as a set. Watch for marking (arrow).

■

The base size of the gear set, measured from the pinion ball bearing to the center of the ring gear is 75,5 ± 0,05 mm (2.97" ± 0.002").

The measurement inscribed on the ring gear and in the housing have to be subtracted from each other.

■

The difference between the two figures has to be inserted as shims between the rear drive housing and the pinion ball bearing (arrow).

■

To adjust the backlash, place an appropriate size brass thrust washer between the needle bearing inner race and the needle bearing of the ring gear.

Adjust ring gear and pinion backlash and ring gear end play according to 33 12 054.

■

33 12 054 Ring gear backlash and end play adjustment

Ring and pinion gear replacement according to 33 12 051

Check backlash and mesh by installing a dial indicator on the outer edge of the ring gear. Use holder, BMW tool No. 5104 and fixture, BMW tool No. 260 (for data see 'Specifications').

Tooth contact pattern check. Check drive side contact of the pinion using 'Prussian Blue'. Correct pattern is in the center of the tooth somewhat closer to the heel (forward end) of the tooth.

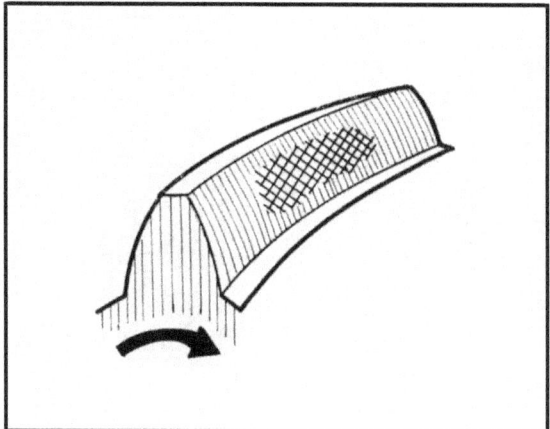

If the contact is too far forward on the tooth (too much on the heel) correct this with a thicker spacer between the pinion bearing and the housing. Subsequently correct the backlash by using a thinner thrust washer between ring gear needle bearing.

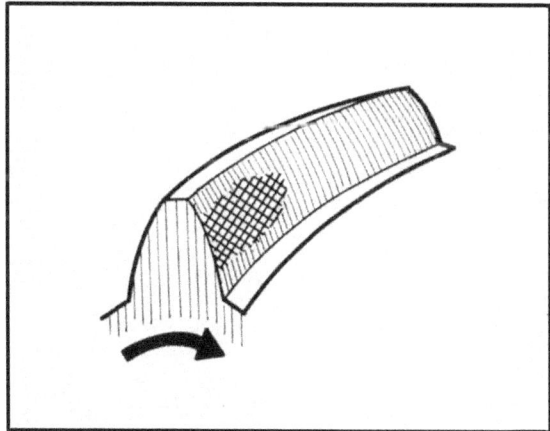

If the tooth contact is too far to the rear (too much on the toe) of the pinion tooth, correct this by using a smaller shim between the pinion bearing and the housing. This will then require a thicker thrust washer between the ring gear needle bearing.
After completion of tooth pattern adjustment check pattern again, also check backlash. Remove and install pinion only when housing is heated.

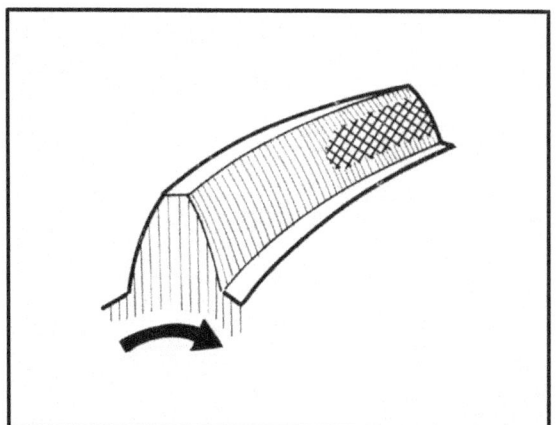

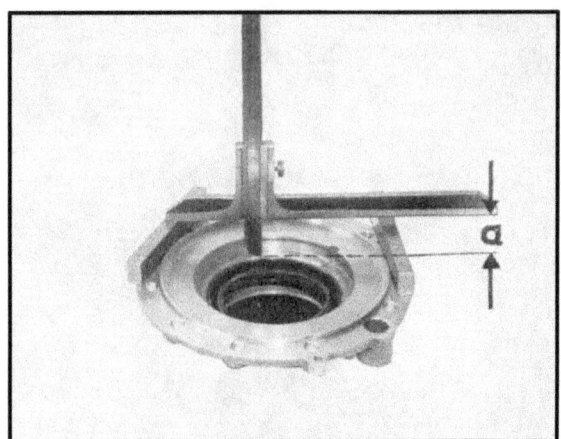

Adjust endplay to '0' without gasket. Use a depth gauge and a pair of prisms, BMW tool No. 50–36, and measure the distance from the ball bearing seat in the cover to the gasket mating surface of the cover (a).

With the ring gear installed in the rear drive housing, measure the distance from the ball bearing to the gasket mating surface of the housing (b). (This is done without the gasket).
By subtracting the distance of measurement 'a' from the distance of measurement 'b' the correct size of the required shims is obtained. The endplay is adjusted '0' without the gasket. The gasket provides the small amount of endplay required.

33 17 350 Swing arm removal and installation

Rear wheel removal according to 36 30 320
Rear drive unit removal according to 33 10 010
Battery removal according to 61 21 010
Rear fender removed according to 46 62 000

Remove the battery bracket holding bolts and remove the left and right battery bracket.
Shock absorber removal according to 33 52 000

Remove drive shaft boot clamp at the transmission and fold boot back as far as possible.

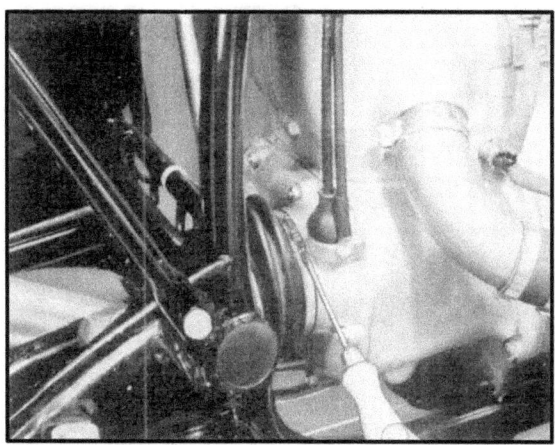

Remove the four drive shaft mounting bolts with a box-end wrench. Lock drive shaft with holder, BMW tool No. 508.

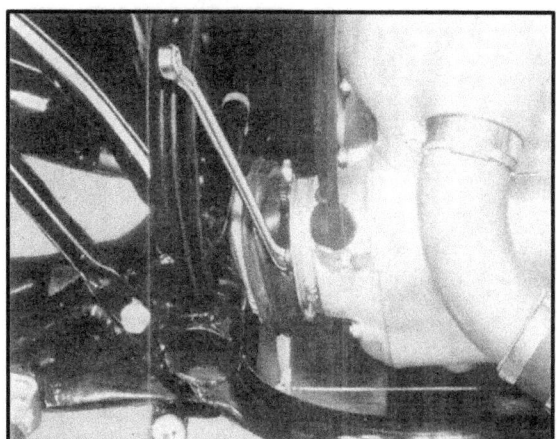

To remove the swing arm pivot pins, remove the dust covers, loosen the lock nuts (1) and remove the privot pins (2).

Assembly instruction: Install pivot pins and center swing arm to have an even distance on both sides (a). Check and ascertain that the drive shaft is centered in the swing arm tube. This is to make sure that it does not touch during full swing arm movement. If necessary, the distance 'a' can be slightly different between both sides.

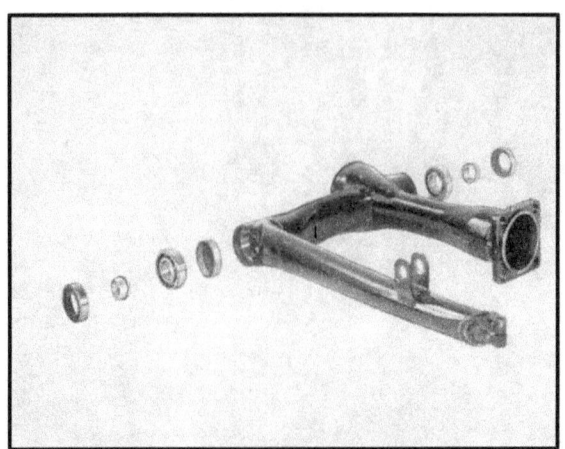

33 17 363 Swing arm disassembly

Swing arm removal according to 33 17 350

Remove seals, thrust spacers, and bearing inner races.
Assembly instruction: Grease bearings before reassembly.

■

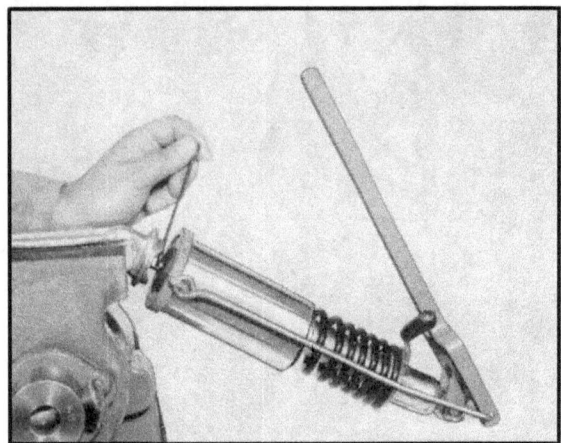

33 52 000 Shock unit removal and installation

Remove hex. nuts and washers and withdraw upper mounting bolts. Before removing the left lower mount bolt slightly elevate the swing arm.
Caution: The Boge Nivomat (option) can not be repaired or tampered with due to its high internal pressure,
Danger. Repairs can only be performed by the manufacturer. When storing this unit make certain that it is stored in an upright position otherwise there is the possibility of a failure.

■

33 52 053 Shock unit disassembly and reassembly

Turn the lever to the lowest tension ('Rider' position). Install shock compressor, BMW tool No. 550, and clamp upper shock unit eye in a vise. Compress the shock unit and withdraw the upper eye from the aluminium cover. Insert an openend wrench on the two flat portions of the shock absorber rod and unscrew the upper eye.

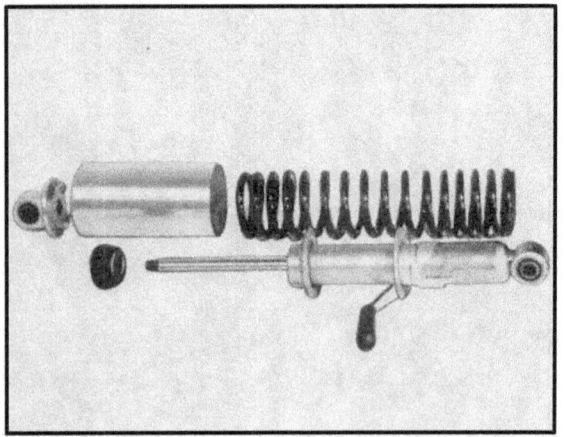

■

Assembly instructions: Reassemble the shock units in the correct sequence, replace the bushings in the upper or lower eye only if necessary.
Before reassembly check the spring length and spring tension (see 'Specifications'). The shock absorber has to have more restriction on extension than on compression, extension and compression movement has to be smooth. If extension and compression is even and the movement is jerky, the shock absorber should be replaced or it is leaking.
Caution: never exert more than one (1) lb. of pressure on a retracted shock absorber.

■

34 Brakes

Specifications . . . . Page 3
34 11 100   Front brake removal and installation 5

Specifications

Brakes

Type	R 50/5	R 60/5	R 75/5
Front wheel brake		Double leading shoe	
Rear wheel brake		Single leading shoe	
Brake drum diameter mm		200 (7.87")	
Brake lining width mm		30 (1.18")	
Lining area cm^2		ca. 107 (16.6 Sq. inches)	
Minimum lining thickness mm		1,5 (0.06")	
Max. allowable run-out of the braking surface to wheel hub mm		0,02 (0.0008")	

34 11 100 Front brake removal and installation

Remove front wheel according to 36 30 300

To remove brake cable from front brake plate, release the adjustment screw sufficiently so that the brake cable retainers can be removed from the two brake levers.

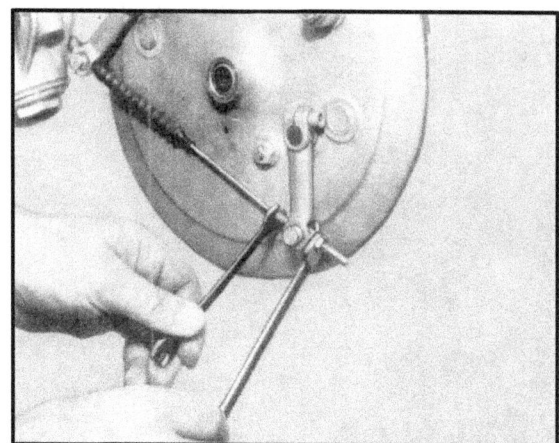

Adjustment of front brake: Adjust hand lever to have a play of 8÷15 mm (0.315÷0.591") by turning the knurled screw after loosening the lock nut. Loosen lock nut of the adjustment cam, turn the cam to the left until it is tight, then turn it back to a point where the lower front brake lever has a free movement of 4 mm (0.157"), measured at the cable anchor, before the shoe is fully applied. Tighten lock nut of adjustment cam. Now adjust the cable, by turning the set screw on cable lower end, to get a free movement of the upper brake lever of 4 mm (0.157") before the upper shoe is fully applied.

Adjustment of foot brake: Turn the wing nut at the end of the brake rod to the right until rear wheel barely starts braking. Then back the wing nut off 3–4 turns.

35 Foot brake lever

35 21 000   Foot brake lever removal and installation   . . . .   Page   3

35 21 000 Foot brake lever removal and installation

Remove the hex. nut and lock washer from the pivot bolt.

Rotate connecting pin to unhook the spring clip and withdraw it.

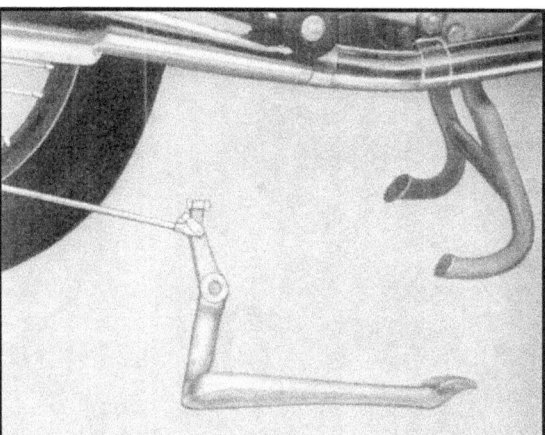

36 Wheels and tires

Specifications	Page	3
36 30 300 Front wheel removal and installation		5
36 30 320 Rear wheel removal and installation		6
36 31 311 Wheel rim replacement (front or rear)		7
36 31 351 Wheel bearing replacement		8

Specifications

Wheels and tires

Type	R 50/5	R 60/5	R 75/5
rim type		aluminum alloy drop-center rims	
rim size front		1,85 B × 19	
rim size rear		1,85 B × 18	
number of spokes per wheel		40	
Radial runout max. mm		0,5 mm (0.02") measured on the outer rim edge	
Lateral runout max. mm		0,2 mm (0.008") measured on the outer rim edge	
Tire size front		3,25 S 19	
Tire size rear		4,00 S 18	
Maximum allowable unbalance on the inner rim diameter cmp in grams g		170 8÷9 (0.28÷0.315 oz.)	
Tire pressure front wheel atü front wheel with passenger atü		1,9 (27 psi) 2,0 (27 psi)	
rear wheel atü rear wheel with passenger atü		1,8 (26 psi) 2,25 (30 psi)	
with tire warm atü		0,3 more (4 psi additional)	
When driving at maximum speeds for longer periods increase the tire inflation by atü		0,2 higher (3 psi)	
Wheel bearing grease		Brand name grease with a drip point of 360° F	

Specifications

Wheels and tires

Type	R 50/5	R 60/5	R 75/5
Permissible wheel load front			
at 27 psi kg		160 (353 lbs.)	
28 psi kg		245 (540 lbs.)	
Permissible wheel load rear			
at 27 psi kg		178 (393 lbs.)	
30 psi kg		270 (595 lbs.)	

Torque specifications mkp (ft/lbs.)

Axle nuts front and rear	4,5÷4,8 (32.5÷34.4)

All other screws and nuts should be tightened following the usual normal values quoted in the tables of the screw firms or in the new BMW standards sheet 60002.1.

36 30 300 Front wheel removal and installation

Put motorcycle on the center stand elevate the front wheel until it is free of the ground by placing a suitable block under the oil pan.

Remove the cotter pin and remove the nut from the allenhead bolt which holds the brake support arm. Withdraw the bolt.

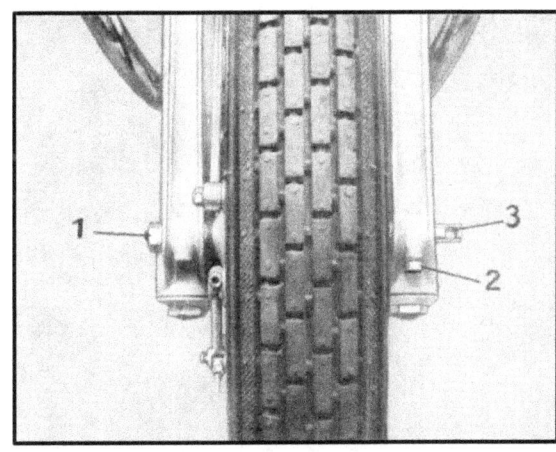

Remove axle nut (1) with washer loosen allenhead clamp bolt (2), and withdraw the axle (3).

Assembly Instructions: Before reassembly, grease the front axle lightly, insert the axle and tighten the axle nut. It necessary, prevent the axle from turning by inserting a pin through the axle. Depress fork several times and then tighten the clamp bolt (2). This prevents the fork from binding.

Roll front wheel out.

36 30 320 Rear wheel removal and installation

Place motorcycle on the center stand and prop up the rear wheel with a suitable block.

■

Remove axle nut and washer.

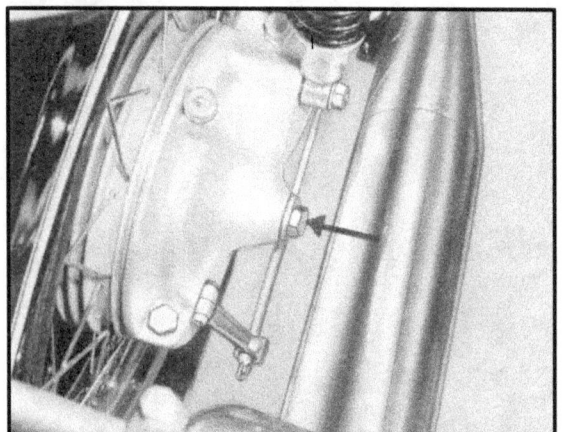

■

Remove clamp bolt on the left swing arm tube, and withdraw the axle.

■

Assembly instructions: Clean the axle and splines; grease lightly with a high drip point grease. Rotate axle during insertion. After tightening the axle nut (1), take the motor cycle from the center stand and depress the rear end several times to prevent binding, then tighten clamp bolt (2)—the hole in the end of the axle (arrow) should be horizontal.

Withdraw wheel from rear drive. To facilitate removal of the wheel lean the motorcycle slightly to the right.

■

36 31 311   Rim replacement (front or rear)

Front wheel removed according to 36 30 300
Rear wheel removed according to 36 30 320

The motorcycles R 50/5, R 60/5 and R 75/5 are equipped with aluminum alloy rims. The rim sizes are, in the front 1.85 B × 19 and in the rear 1.85 B × 18. To install the rims, the spoke gauges BMW tool No. 251 for rear wheel and BMW tool No. 252 for front wheel are necessary. Replacement brake drums have an undersized inner diameter. After the wheel is spoked-in, the drum has to be turned on a lathe to the size of 200, plus 0.185 mm (7.874", plus 0.072"). For this, support the hub in the center and turn the drum to a fine finish. This removes the distortion caused by the lacing process. Maximum allowable run-out of the brake drum to the hub is 0,02 mm (0.00078"). Place wheel hub on a bench with the drum side down. Insert a pair of spokes with retainers into the hub. Note, the holes in the hub are not on the same level.

Install the rim. Place the marking on the inside of the rim on the open side of the brake drum, so that the arrow points in the direction of rotation. The nipple depression in the rim must point in the same direction as the spoke. The higher situated spoke must meet the higher nipple hole in the rim. The lower spoke will then meet the lower hole in the rim. The remaining spokes are inserted in the same fashion.

All spoke nipples are tightened evenly.
Place the rim with axle into balancing fixture, BMW tool No. 5106.
Previously, slide onto thinner side of axle, the spacer sleeve, BMW tool No. 251 for rear wheel, and BMW tool No. 252 for front wheel.

Assembly instruction: Grease spoke nipple thread lightly before installation.

Maximum allowable radial run-out (checks taken on the rim edge) see specifications.

Caution: Grind down protruding spoke ends to prevent damage to the inner tube.
Retighten the spokes after 1200 miles. All wheels must be balanced after tire installation.

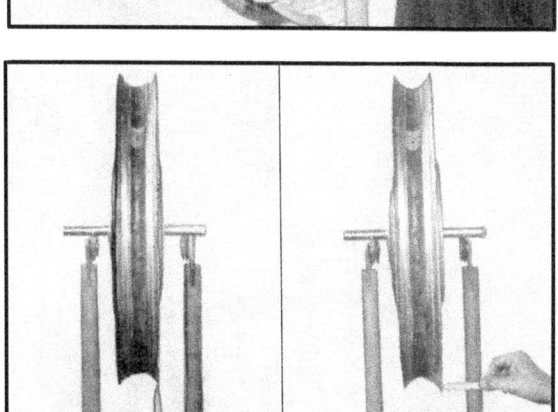

8. 69

Balancing wheels statically:

Install wheels with axle into balancing fixture, BMW tool No. 5106.
Previously, slide on thinner side of axle, the spacer sleeve, BMW tool No. 553 on front wheel or BMW tool No. 554 on rear wheel (arrow).

■

Wait until wheel is at standstill, then tap corrective weights with a hammer onto spokes situated above. A correctly balanced wheel must stand still in any position. Maximum allowable unbalance see specifications.

■

36 31 351 Replacement of wheel bearings (front or rear)

Front wheel removed according to 36 30 300
Rear wheel removed according to 36 30 320

Remove hex head bolts with lock washer. Remove hub cap.

■

Remove bearing cover plate with seal and thrust sleeve. Withdraw bearing inner race with cage, spacer ring, and inner spacer sleeve. (On the front wheel first remove the reducing sleeve). Insert drift, BMW tool No. 5074, into spacer sleeve on the side of the brake drum and tap out left bearing outer race, outer spacer sleeve, bearing on the side of the brake, and right spacer sleeve.

■

46 Frame

Specifications	Page	3
46 52 000 Center stand removal and installation		5
46 53 000 Sidestand removal and installation		6
46 61 000 Front fender removal and installation		7
46 62 000 Rear fender removal and installation		8

Specifications

Frame

	R 50/5	R 60/5	R 75/5
Type			
Frame	Double loop tubular frame with oval tubing in areas of high stress with bolted on rear section. Not suited for side car operation.		
Location of identification plate	on the steering head		
Location of serial number	on the right side of the steering head		
Weights and dimensions			
Over all width engine mm	740 (29.1")		
Over all height without mirror mm (without load)	1100 (44")		
Seat height (without load) mm	850 (33.5")		
Over all length mm	2100 (82.7")		
Wheel base mm	1385 (54.5")		
Ground clearance with load of a rider weighing 165 lbs. mm	165 (6.5")		
Curb weight, including lubricants, but without fuel and tools kg	185 (408 lbs.)	190 (419 lbs.)	190 (419 lbs.)
Curb weight including lubricants fuel and tools kg	205 (452 lbs.)	210 (463 lbs.)	210 (463 lbs.)
Permissible total weight curb weight plus two people and luggage kg	398 (881 lbs.)		
Permissible wheel load front at 27 psi tire pressure (lbs) kg	160 (353 lbs.)		
28 kg	178		
28 kg	245 (540 lbs.)		
30 kg	270		
Maximum load including operator	2 people		

8.69

Specifications

Frame

Type	R 50/5	R 60/5	R 75/5

Torque specifications mkp (ft/lbs)

Rear frame section mounting bolts	2,5 (18.0)	Center stand bolts	3,5 (25.3)
Nuts for upper front fender brace	2,3 (16.6)	Nuts for lower front fender brace	0,25 (1.8)

All other screws and nuts should be tightened following the usual normal values quoted in the tables of the screw firms or in the new BMW standards sheet 60002.1.

46 52 000 Center stand removal and installation

Place a suitable block under the oil pan and raise the motorcycle until the center stand does not touch the ground.

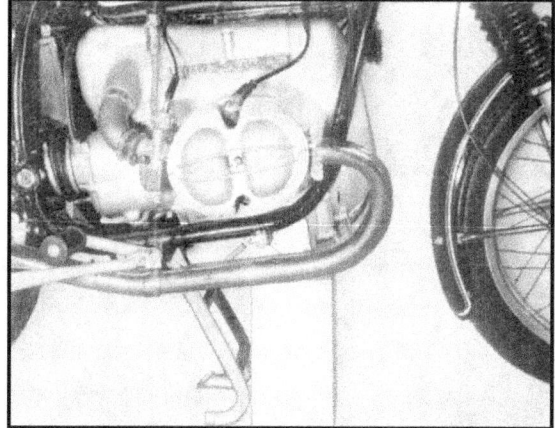

Unhook the left and right center stand return springs.

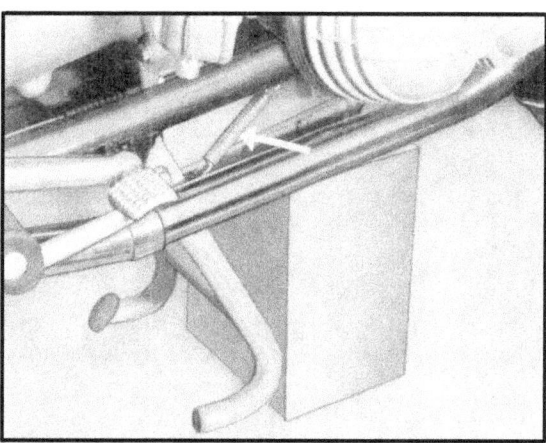

Remove hex head bolt (left and right) (arrow) and withdraw center stand to the rear. Watch for the spacers.

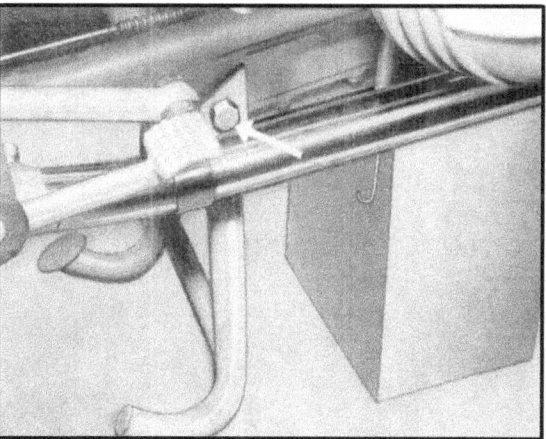

46 53 000 Side stand removal and installation

Unhook side stand return spring.

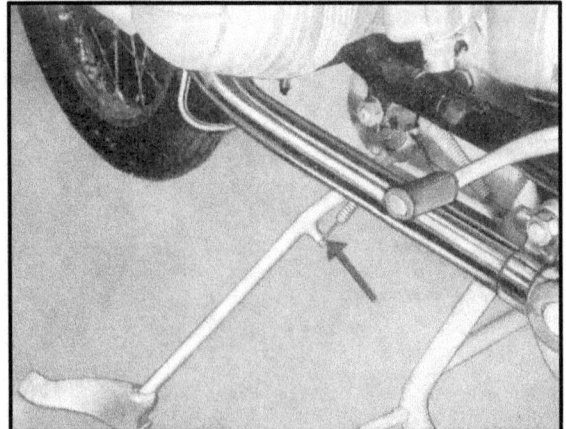

■

Drive out retainer pin (arrow) with an appropriate drift and withdraw sidestand.

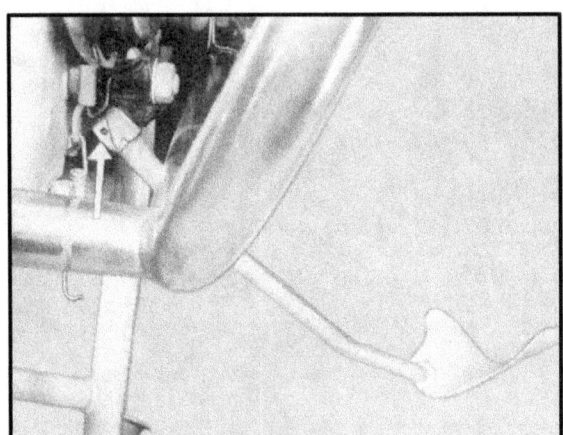

■

46 61 000 Front fender removal and installation

Front wheel removal according to 36 30 300

Remove the four self locking nuts of the upper fender brace.

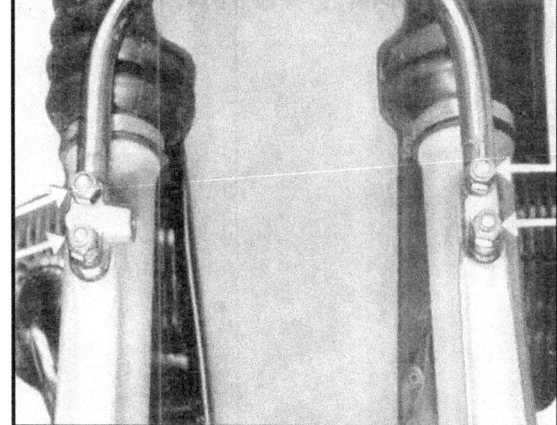

Remove the two nuts bolts and lock washers of the lower center brace.

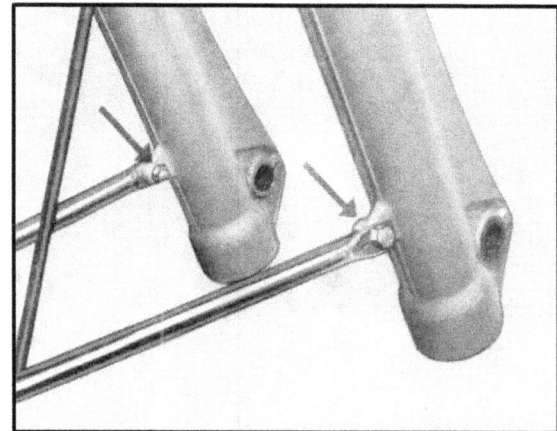

Assembly Instructions
During reassembly, insert upper fender brace on the four studs of the fork legs, and attach lower fender brace loosely on the fork legs. Tighten the fender brace after the wheel and front brake plate is completely installed and tightened (for torque see Specifications).

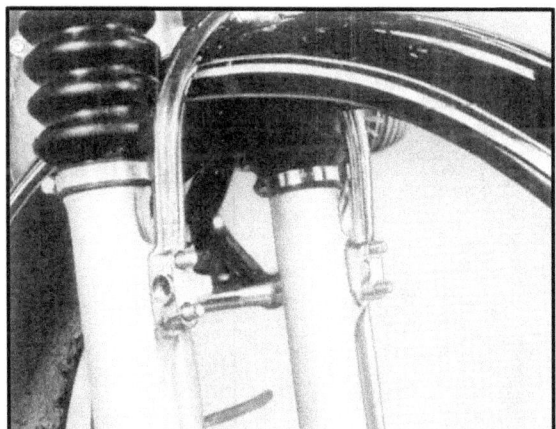

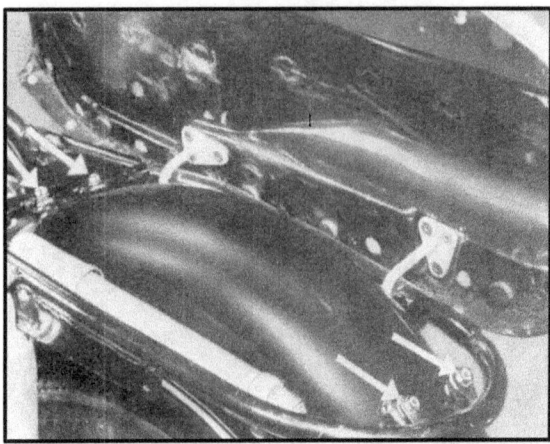

46 62 000   Rear fender removal and installation

Disconnect the negative battery cable.
Flip open the dual seat, remove the four hex head bolts with washers, rubber spacers, and self locking nuts (arrow).

Remove the lower mounting bolts with self locking nuts from the frame.

Remove the 2 Philipps head screws from the tail light and remove the tail light lens and reflector.

Remove the 2 bolts nuts and washers (arrow) and remove tail light housing and turn signal carrier from the fender.

52 Dual seat

52 53 000   Dual seat removal and installation . . . .   Page   3

52 53 000 Dual seat removal and installation

Flip open dual seat.

Remove the 3 allenhead bolts (arrow) and withdraw dual seat to the rear.

61 Frame electrical system

Specifications and wiring diagram	Page	3
61 21 010 Battery removal and installation		7
61 31 350 Turn signal flasher removal and installation		7
61 33 000 Horn removal and installation		7

Specifications

Frame electrical system

	R 50/5	R 60/5	R 75/5
Type			
Horn Type		Bosch 0320 123 013 – 12 V – 400 HZ oder Hella B 31 – 12	
Battery Volt		12	
Capacity Ah		15 ampere hours	
Ground		negative	
Lowest voltage required for starting		3	
Turn signal flasher		Hella 91 M 2 E 2×21 W – 12 V	

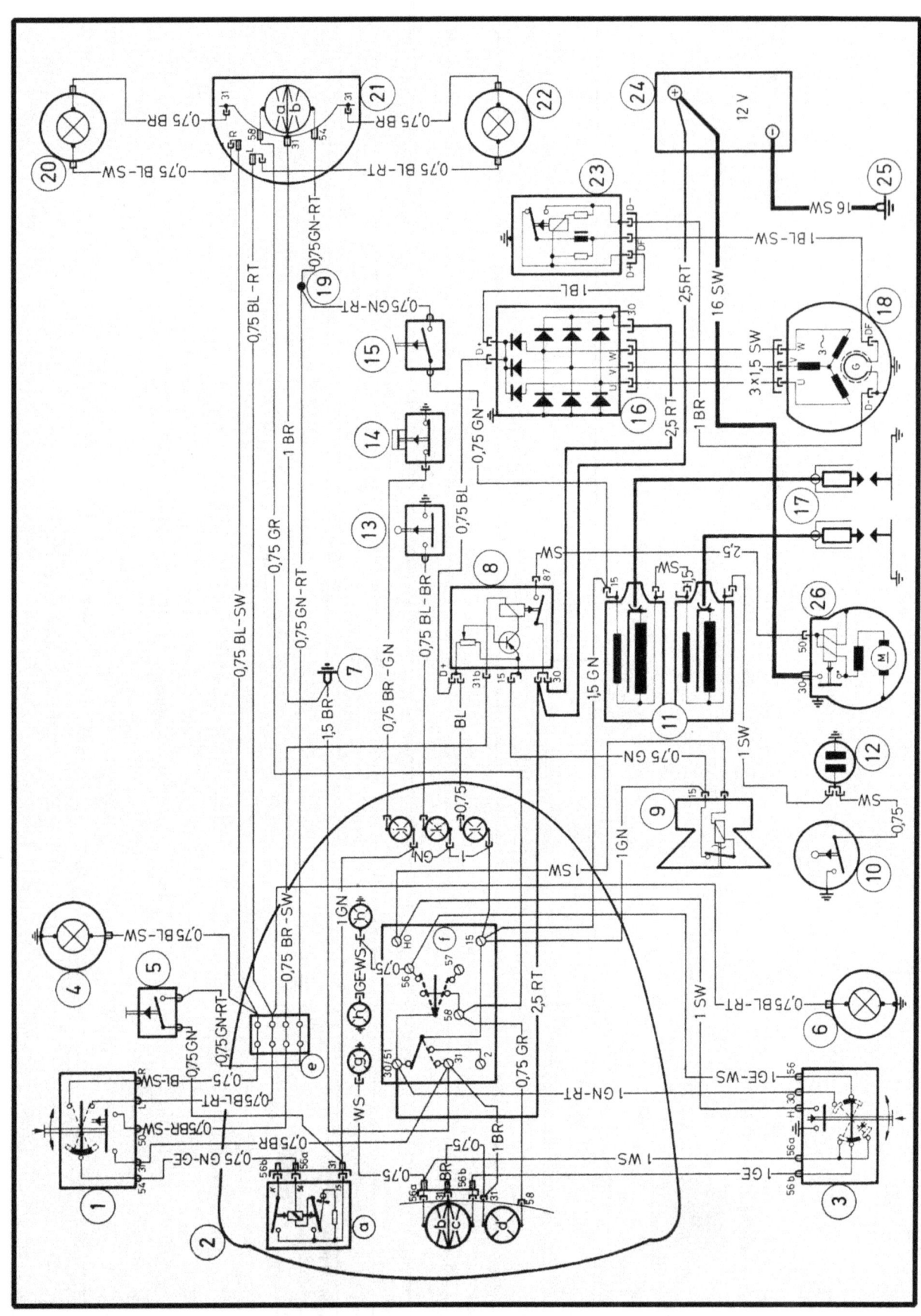

Wiring diagram

1 Turnsignal switch
2 Head-light
  a) Turnsignal flasher
  b) High beam
  c) Low beam
  d) Parking light
  e) Connector plug
  f) Ignition and light switch
  g) High beam indicator (blue)
  h) Instrument illumination
  i) Oil pressure warning (amber)
  k) Transmission neutral indicator (green)
  l) Charging indicator (red)
3 Dimmer switch
4 Turnsignal, front right
5 Front brake-light switch
6 Turnsignal, front left
7 Ground to the frame at the ignition coils
8 Starter protection relay
9 Horn
10 Ignition breaker
11 Ignition coils
12 Condensor
13 Transmission neutral switch
14 Oil pressure warning
15 Rear brake-light switch
16 Diode chassis
17 Spark plugs and spark plug caps
18 Alternator
19 Connections on the wiring harness
20 Turnsignal, right rear
21 Tail/stop light
  a) Tail light and license plate illumination
  b) Stoplight
22 Turnsignal, left rear
23 Regulator
24 Battery
25 Ground wire on transmission cover
26 Starter

Identification

Bl = Blue   GR = Gray   SW = Black
BR = braun   GN = Green   WS = White
GE = yellow   RT = Red

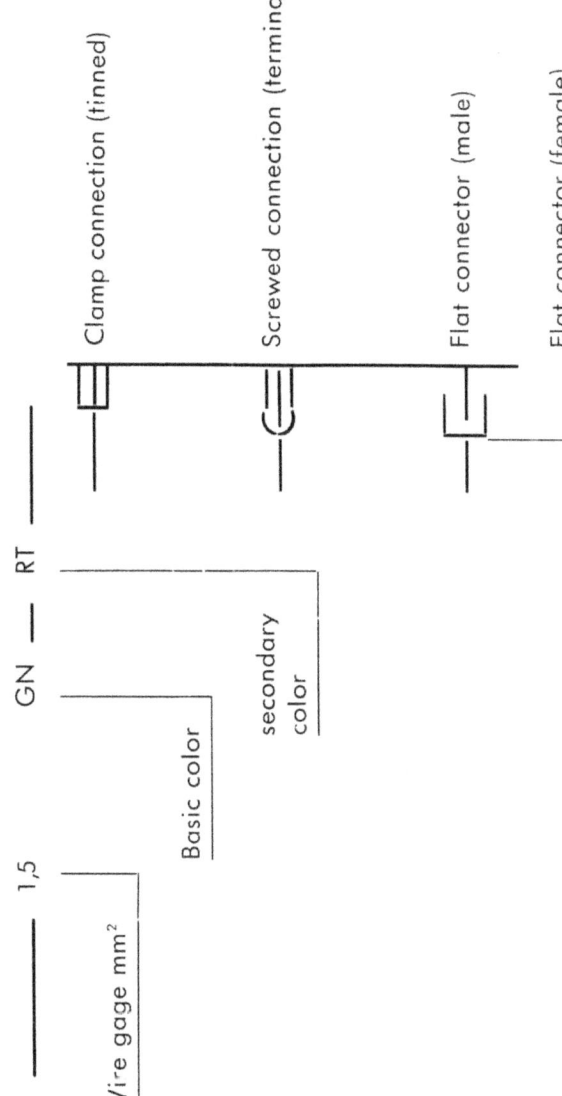

GN — RT

Basic color — secondary color

1,5 — Wire gage mm²

Clamp connection (tinned)
Screwed connection (terminal)
Flat connector (male)
Flat connector (female)

61 21 010 Battery removal and installation

Air filter removal according to 13 72 000

Unhook battery straps. Remove battery cover, disconnect battery cables and withdraw battery to the left.

Assembly Instructions
Insert battery vent tube into the hole provided in the frame (arrow).

61 31 350 Turn signal flasher removal and installation

Disconnect negative battery cable.
Separate head light rim from headlight housing with a screw driver, withdraw flasher from the socket (arrow).

61 33 000 Horn removal and installation

Disconnect negative battery cable.
Remove hex. nut (arrow) from the horn.

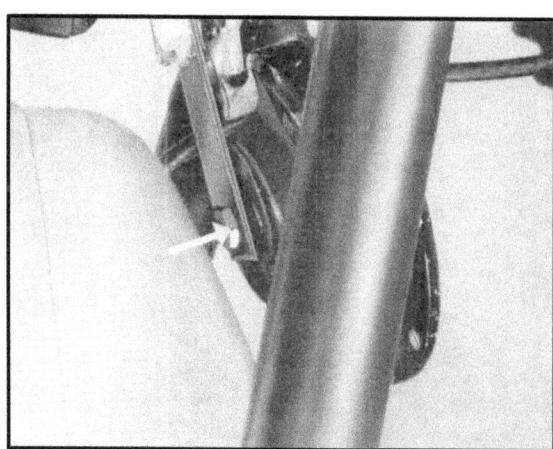

Withdraw horn wires
1 = black wires
2 = two green wires

62 Instruments

Specifications . . . . Page 3
62 11 000 Instrument cluster removal and installation 5
62 11 020 Speedometer cable removal and installation 5

Instruments

Specifications

Type	R 50/5	R 60/5	R 75/5
Speedometer ratio km	0,811	0,766	0,665
Speedometer ratio Miles	1,297	1,226	1,0625
Speed indication km		20÷200	
Speed indication Miles		10÷120	

62 11 000 Intrument cluster removal and installation

Disconnect negative cable from the battery.
Separate headlight rim from the headlight housing with a screw driver. Withdraw flasher unit and indicator lamps.
Remove the speedometer cable (1) tachometer cable (2) and the 2 serrated nuts (3).

Withdraw instrument cluster from the top.

62 11 020 Speedometer cable removal and installation

Disconnect negative battery cable.
Separate headlight rim from head light housing with a screw driver.
Withdraw the flasher unit and indicator lamps.
Remove speedometer cable from the instrument cluster.

Remove the speedometer cable rubber grommet.

Remove the fuel tank according to 16 11 030

Pull back the cable boot at the transmission, remove the cable clamp bolt and remove the negative battery cable and washer. Withdraw the speedometer cable.

Assembly Instructions

Route the speedometer cable on the frame exactly as shown in the picture (arrow).

63 Lighting

Specifications	Page	3
63 10 004	Headlight aim adjustment	5
63 21 180	Tail/stop light removal and installation	6
63 23 000	Turnsignal removal and installation	7
63 99 101	Headlight bulb replacement	8
63 99 271	Turnsignal bulb replacement	9
63 99 341	Tail light bulb replacement	9

Specifications

Lighting

Type	R 50/5	R 60/5	R 75/5
Headlight		Bosch 0 303 550 002	
High and low beam		12 V 45/40 W Double filament bulb	
Parking light		12 V 4 W Parking lamp	
Transmission neutral indicator lamp		12 V 2 W Indicator lamp	
Charging indicator lamp (red)		12 V 4 W Indicator lamp	
Oil pressure indicator lamp (amber)		12 V 2 W Indicator lamp	
High beam indicator lamp (blue)		12 V 2 W Indicator lamp	
Instrument illumination		12 V 2 W	
Tail light and license plate illumination / Stoplight		12 V 5 W / 12 V 21 W Double filament bulb	
Turnsignal lamps (front and rear, two each)		12 V 21 W Bulb (RL)	

63 10 004   Headlight adjustment

If any work is performed on the headlight it is necessary to subsequently adjust the headlight aim. Proceed as follows:

Check tire pressure and correct if necessary.
Place motorcycle on its wheels with the rider aboard on a level surface 16½ feet from a light colored wall. The rear springs should be set for solo operation. Measure the distance from the floor to headlight center. Mark this distance on the wall with a cross and draw another cross 2" below the first one. Turn on low beam and align the headlight so that the dark boundary runs from the left from the center of the lower cross rising to the right to the horizontal line of the upper cross and then falls off.

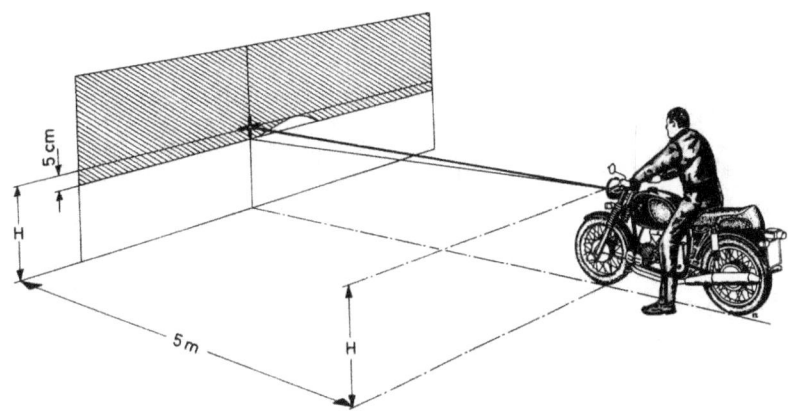

63 21 180 Tail/Stop light removal and installation

Disconnect negative battery cable, remove the 2 screws holding the tail light lens and remove the lens.

■

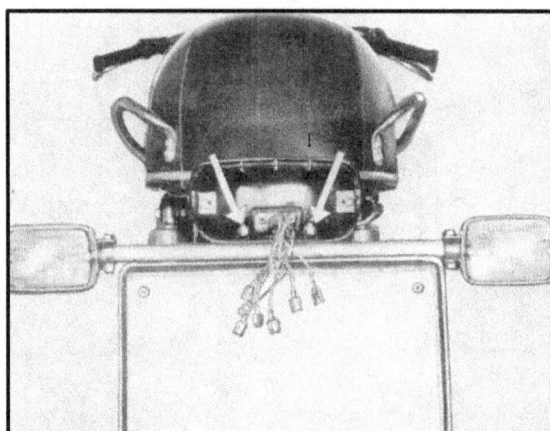

Withdraw the tail light wires from the reflector. Note the color of the wires.

Remove the 2 taillight mount bolts and nuts and remove the housing.

Assembly Instructions
Make certain that license plate illumination faces downward when installing the taillight lens.

■

63 23 000 Turnsignal unit removal and installation (one unit front or rear)

Disconnect negative battery cable.
Remove the 2 Philipps head screws and remove the turn signal lens.

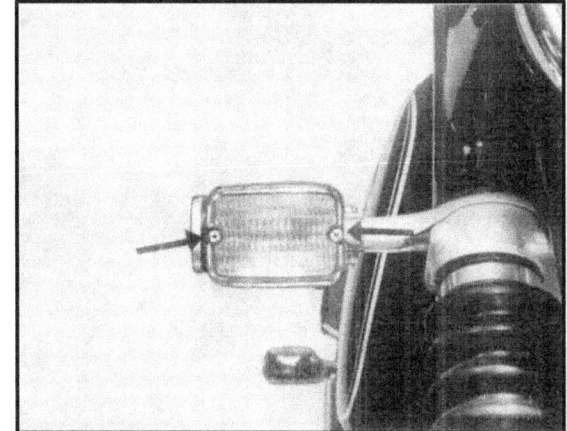

Disconnect the wire from the turn signal reflector (arrow).

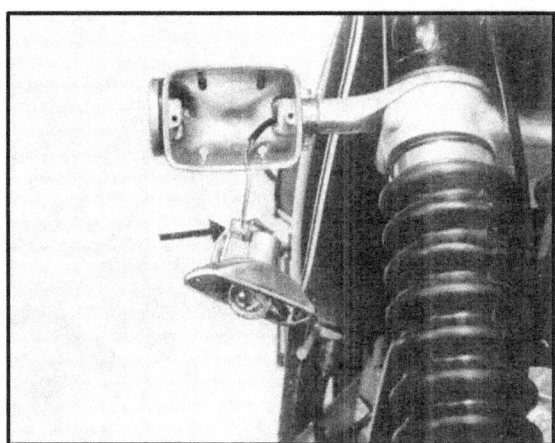

Loosen the clamp bolt and withdraw the turn signal housing.

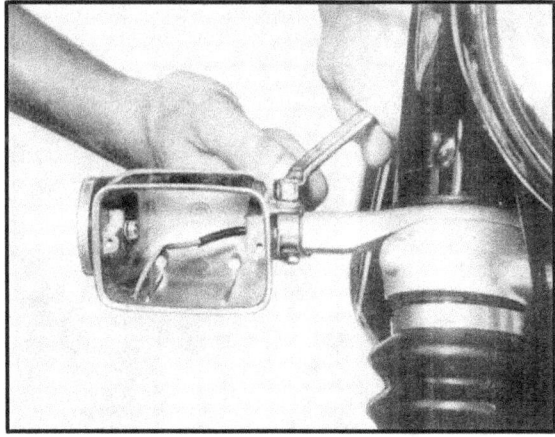

Assembly Instructions

When installing the turn signal lens, make certain that the designation "TOP" is on the top.

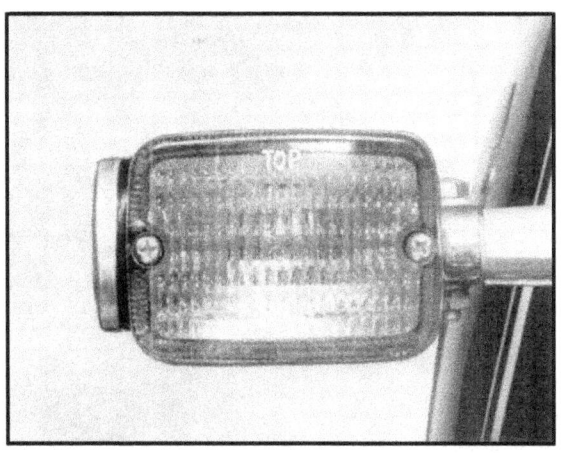

63 99 101   Headlight bulb replacement

Disconnect the negative battery cable. Separate the headlight rim from the headlight housing with a screw driver.

■

Remove the bayonet type bulb holder from the reflector by turning it.

Remove the double-filament bulb.

Assembly Instructions
When inserting the headlight bulb, make sure that locating tab of the bulb fits into the recess of the reflector.

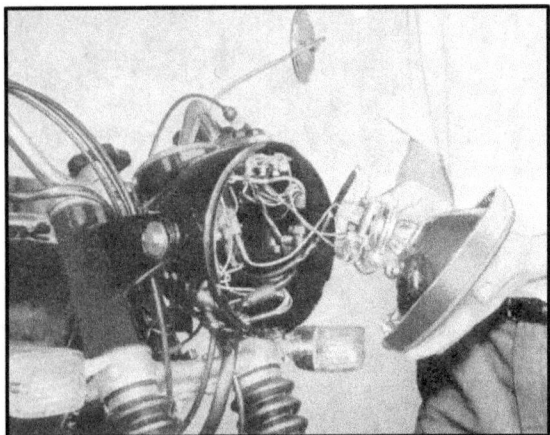

■

The parking light bulb is inserted into the reflector through the headlight bulb opening.

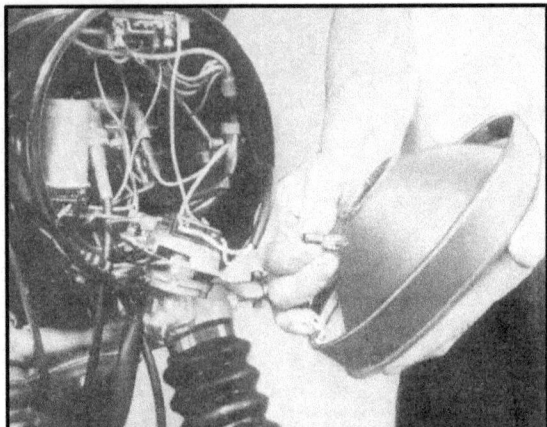

■

63 99 271 Turn signal bulb replacement (front or rear)

Disconnect negative battery cable.
Remove both Philips head screws and remove turn signal lens.

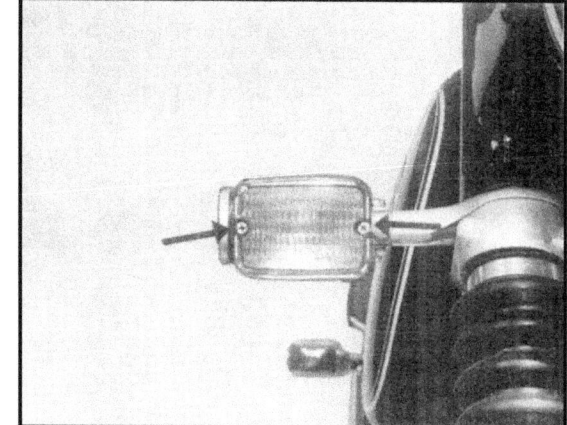

Remove bulb from reflector by pushing it in slightly and turning it to the left. It can then be withdrawn.

Assembly Instructions
When installing the turn signal lens, make certain that the designation "TOP" is placed at the top.

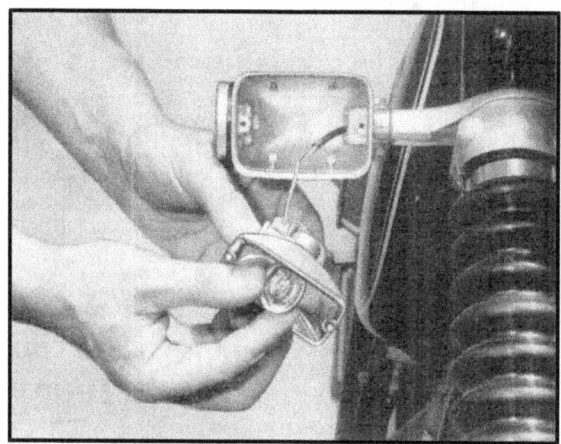

63 99 341 Tail light bulb replacement

Disconnect negative battery cable.
Loosen the 2 Philipps head screws and remove the tail light lens.

Remove the bulb from the reflector by pressing it in lightly and turning it to the left. It can then be withdrawn.

Assembly Instructions
When installing the tail light lens, make certain that the license plate illumination faces downward.

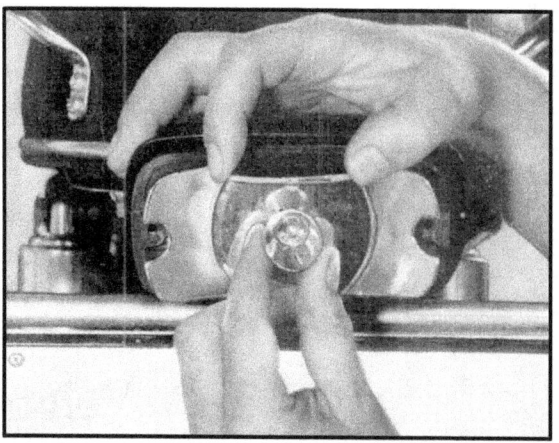

8. 69

VELOCEPRESS MANUALS – MOTORCYCLE BY MAKE

AJS 1932-1948 SINGLES & TWINS 250cc THRU 1000cc (BOOK OF)
AJS 1945-1960 SINGLES 350cc & 500cc MODELS 16 & 18 (BOOK OF)
AJS 1955-1965 SINGLES 350cc & 500cc (BOOK OF)
AJS 1957-1966 FACTORY WSM - ALL SINGLES & TWINS
ARIEL UP TO 1932 (BOOK OF)
ARIEL 1932-1939 PREWAR MODELS (BOOK OF)
ARIEL 1933-1951 (WORKSHOP MANUAL)
ARIEL 1939-1960 4 STROKE SINGLES (BOOK OF)
ARIEL 1958-1964 LEADER & ARROW FACTORY WSM & PARTS LIST
ARIEL 1958-1964 LEADER & ARROW (BOOK OF)
BMW R26 R27 (1956-1967) FACTORY WORKSHOP MANUAL
BMW R50 R50S R60 R69S (1955-1969) FACTORY WORKSHOP MANUAL
BMW R50/5 R60/5 R75/5 (1969-1973) FACTORY WORKSHOP MANUAL
BRIDGESTONE 90 SERIES FACTORY WSM & PARTS CATALOGUE
BRIDGESTONE 175 SERIES FACTORY WSM & PARTS CATALOGUE
BRIDGESTONE 350 SERIES FACTORY WSM & PARTS CATALOGUE
BSA SERVICE SHEETS MASTER CATALOGUE ALL MODELS 1945-1967
BSA BANTAM D1 TO D7 1948-1966 FACTORY SERVICE SHEETS MANUAL
BSA BANTAM ALL MODELS FROM 1948 ONWARDS (BOOK OF)
BSA BANTAM D14 FACTORY SERVICE MANUAL
BSA DANDY FACTORY WORKSHOP MANUAL (COMPILATION)
BSA SINGLES & V-TWINS UP TO 1926 inc. 1927 SUPPLEMENT (BOOK OF)
BSA SINGLES & V-TWINS UP TO 1930 (BOOK OF)
BSA SINGLES & V-TWINS UP TO 1935 (BOOK OF)
BSA SINGLES & V-TWINS 1936-1939 (BOOK OF)
BSA C10, C11 & C12 1945-1958 FACTORY SERVICE SHEETS MANUAL
BSA OHV & SV SINGLES 250-600cc 1945-1959 (BOOK OF)
BSA C15 & B40 1958-1967 FACTORY SERVICE SHEETS MANUAL
BSA OHV & SV SINGLES 250cc (ONLY) 1954-1970 (BOOK OF)
BSA B31, B32, B33 & B34 1945-60 FACTORY SERVICE SHEETS MANUAL
BSA OHV SINGLES 350 & 500cc 1955-1967 (BOOK OF)
BSA M20, M21 & M33 1945-1963 FACTORY SERVICE SHEETS MANUAL
BSA TWINS A7 & A10 1948-1962 FACTORY SERVICE SHEETS MANUAL
BSA TWINS A7 & A10 1948-1962 (BOOK OF)
BSA TWINS A50 & A65 1962-1965 FACTORY WORKSHOP MANUAL
BSA TWINS A50 & A65 1962-1969 (SECOND BOOK OF)
DOUGLAS 1929-1939 PREWAR ALL MODELS (BOOK OF)
DOUGLAS 1948-1957 POSTWAR ALL MODELS FACTORY SHOP MANUAL
DUCATI 160cc, 250cc & 350cc OHC MODELS FACTORY SHOP MANUAL
HONDA 50cc ALL MODELS UP TO 1970 INC MONKEY & TRAIL (BOOK OF)
HONDA 90cc ALL MODELS UP TO 1966 (BOOK OF)
HONDA TWINS & SINGLES 50cc THRU 305cc 1960-1966 (BOOK OF)
HONDA TWINS ALL MODELS 125cc THRU 450cc UP TO 1968 (BOOK OF)
HONDA C100 50cc SUPER CUB O.H.C. 1959-1962 FACTORY WSM
HONDA C110 50cc SPORT CUB O.H.C. 1960-1962 FACTORY WSM
HONDA 50-65-70-90cc O.H.C. SINGLES 1959-1983 FACTORY WSM
HONDA 100-125cc SINGLES CB/CD/CL/SL/TL 1970-1984 FACTORY WSM
HONDA 125-150cc TWINS C/CS/CD/CA 1959-1966 FACTORY WSM
HONDA 125-160-175-200cc TWINS 1965-1978 WORKSHOP MANUAL
HONDA 250-305cc TWINS C/CS/CB 1961-1968 FACTORY WSM
HOHDA 250-350cc TWINS CB/CL/SL 1968-1973 FACTORY WSM
HONDA 250-360cc TWINS CB/CL/CJ 1974-1977 FACTORY WSM
HONDA 350F & 400F 4-CYLINDER 1972-1977 FACTORY WSM
HONDA 450cc TWINS CB/CL 1965-1974 K0 to K7 WORKSHOP MANUAL
HONDA 500cc & 550cc 4-CYL 1971-1978 FACTORY WORKSHOP MANUAL
HONDA 750cc SHOC 4-CYL 1969-1978 K0~K8 WORKSHOP MANUAL
INDIAN PONYBIKE, BOY RACER & PAPOOSE ILL PARTS LIST & SALES LIT

J.A.P. ENGINES 1927-1952 & MOTORCYCLES 1934-1952 (BOOK OF)
MATCHLESS 1931-1939 ALL MODELS 250cc THRU 990cc (BOOK OF)
MATCHLESS 1945-1956 350 & 500cc SINGLES (BOOK OF)
MATCHLESS 1955-1966 350 & 500cc SINGLES (BOOK OF)
MATCHLESS 1957-1966 FACTORY WSM - ALL SINGLES & TWINS
NEW IMPERIAL ALL SV & OHV FROM 1935 ONWARDS (BOOK OF)
NORTON 1932-1939 PREWAR MODELS (BOOK OF)
NORTON 1932-1947 (BOOK OF)
NORTON 1938-1956 (BOOK OF)
NORTON 1945-1963 MODELS 16H, Big4, ES2, 19 & 50 WSM'S & PARTS
NORTON 1955-1963 MODELS 19, 50 & ES2 (BOOK OF)
NORTON 1948-1970 DOMINATOR TWINS FACTORY WSM'S & PARTS
NORTON 1955-1965 DOMINATOR TWINS (BOOK OF)
NORTON 1960-1970 TWIN CYLINDER FACTORY WORKSHOP MANUAL
NORTON 1970-1975 COMMANDO 850 & 750cc FACTORY WSM
NORTON 1975-1978 MK 3 COMMANDO 850 cc FACTORY WSM
PANTHER 1932-1958 LIGHTWEIGHT MODELS 250 & 350cc (BOOK OF)
PANTHER 1938-1966 HEAVYWEIGHT MODELS 600 & 650cc (BOOK OF)
RALEIGH MOTORCYCLES 1919-1933 (BOOK OF)
ROYAL ENFIELD 1934-1946 SINGLES & V TWINS (BOOK OF)
ROYAL ENFIELD 1937-1953 SINGLES & V TWINS (BOOK OF)
ROYAL ENFIELD 1946-1962 SINGLES (BOOK OF)
ROYAL ENFIELD 1948-1963 500cc TWINS FACTORY WORKSHOP MANUAL
ROYAL ENFIELD 1952-1963 700cc TWINS FACTORY WORKSHOP MANUAL
ROYAL ENFIELD 1956-1966 250cc CRUSADER & 350cc NEW BULLET WSM
ROYAL ENFIELD 1958-1966 250cc & 350cc SINGLES (SECOND BOOK OF)
ROYAL ENFIELD 1962-1970 INTERCEPTOR WSM'S & PARTS (Compilation)
RUDGE 1933-1939 (BOOK OF)
SACHS 1968-1975 100cc & 125cc ENGINES WSM & M/CYCLE PARTS LIST
SUNBEAM 1928-1939 (BOOK OF)
SUNBEAM 1946-1957 S7 & S8 (BOOK OF)
SUZUKI 50cc & 80cc UP TO 1966 (BOOK OF)
SUZUKI T10 1963-1967 FACTORY WORKSHOP MANUAL
SUZUKI T20 & T200 1965-1969 FACTORY WORKSHOP MANUAL
SUZUKI TWINS 1962 ONWARDS 125-500cc WORKSHOP MANUAL
TRIUMPH 1935-1949 SINGLES & TWINS (BOOK OF)
TRIUMPH 1937-1961 SINGLES SV & OHV 250cc-600cc + TERRIER & CUB
TRIUMPH 1945-1955 PRE-UNIT 350cc, 500cc & 650cc TWINS WSM No.11
TRIUMPH 1945-1959 TWINS (BOOK OF)
TRIUMPH 1956-1969 TWINS (BOOK OF)
TRIUMPH 1956-1962 PRE-UNIT 500cc & 650cc TWINS WSM No.17
TRIUMPH 1957-1963 UNIT CONSTRUCTION 350-500cc WSM No.4
TRIUMPH 1963-1974 UNIT CONSTRUCTION 350-500cc FACTORY WSM
TRIUMPH 1963-1970 UNIT CONSTRUCTION 650cc FACTORY WSM
TRIUMPH 1968-1974 TRIDENT T150 & T150V FACTORY WSM
TRIUMPH 1971-1973 650cc OIL-IN-FRAME FACTORY WSM
TRIUMPH 1973-1978 750cc BONNEVILLE & TIGER FACTORY WSM
TRIUMPH 1979-1983 750cc T140, TR7 & TR65 FACTORY WSM
VELOCETTE 1925-1970 ALL SINGLES & TWINS (BOOK OF)
VELOCETTE 1933-1952 MOV-MAC-MSS RIGID FRAME FACTORY WSM
VELOCETTE 1954-1971 MSS-VENOM-THRUXTON-VIPER FACTORY WSM
VILLIERS ENGINE UP TO 1959 INC. 3 WHEELERS (BOOK OF)
VILLIERS ENGINE UP TO 1969 (BOOK OF)
VINCENT 1935-1955 (WORKSHOP MANUAL)
YAMAHA 1961-1967 YA5 & YA6 (WORKSHOP MANUAL & ILL PARTS LIST)
YAMAHA 1971-1972 JT1& JT2 (WORKSHOP MANUAL & ILL PARTS LIST)

VELOCEPRESS MANUALS – SCOOTERS BY MAKE

BSA SUNBEAM SCOOTER WORKSHOP MANUAL 1959-1965
BSA SUNBEAM SCOOTER 1959-1965 (BOOK OF)
LAMBRETTA 1947-1957 ALL 125 & 150cc MODELS (BOOK OF)
LAMBRETTA 1957-1970 LI & TV MODELS (SECOND BOOK OF)
NSU PRIMA 1956-1964 ALL MODELS (BOOK OF)
TRIUMPH TIGRESS SCOOTER WORKSHOP MANUAL 1959-1965
TRIUMPH TIGRESS SCOOTER (BOOK OF)
VESPA 1951-1961 (BOOK OF)
VESPA 1955-1963 125 & 150cc & GS MODELS (SECOND BOOK OF)
VESPA 1955-1968 GS & SS (BOOK OF)
VESPA 1963-1972 90, 125 & 150cc (THIRD BOOK OF)

VELOCEPRESS MANUALS – MOPEDS & MOTORIZED BICYCLES

CYCLEMOTOR (BOOK OF)
NSU QUICKLY 1953-1963 ALL MODELS (BOOK OF)
PUCH MAXI N & S MAINTENANCE & REPAIR (3 MANUAL COMPILATION)
RALEIGH MOPEDS 1960-1969 (BOOK OF)

VELOCEPRESS MANUALS - THREE WHEELER'S

BOND MINICAR THREE WHEELER 1948-1967 (BOOK OF)
BMW ISETTA FACTORY WORKSHOP MANUAL
BSA THREE WHEELER (BOOK OF)
RELIANT REGAL THREE WHEELER 1952-1973 (BOOK OF)
VINTAGE MORGAN THREE WHEELER (BOOK OF)

VELOCEPRESS TECHNICAL BOOKS – MOTORCYCLE

1930'S BRITISH MOTORCYCLE CARBS & ELEC COMPONENTS (BOOK OF)
1930'S BRITISH MOTORCYCLE ENGINES (OVERHAUL & MAINTENANCE)
1930'S BRITISH MOTORCYCLE GEARBOXES & CLUTCHES (BOOK OF)
CATALOG OF BRITISH MOTORCYCLES (1951 MODELS)
LUCAS ELECTRONICS BRITISH M/CYCLES REPAIR & PARTS (1950-1977)
MOTORCYCLE ENGINEERING (P.E. Irving)
MOTORCYCLE ROAD TESTS 1949-1953 (Motor Cycle Magazine UK)
SPEED AND HOW TO OBTAIN IT (Motor Cycle Magazine UK)
TUNING FOR SPEED (P.E. Irving)
WIPAC (COMBO) MANUAL NUMBER 3 + M/CYCLE & SCOOTER MANUAL

For Automobile manuals and books
Please visit our website
VelocePress.com

www.ingramcontent.com/pod-product-compliance
Lightning Source LLC
Chambersburg PA
CBHW080733300426

44114CB00019B/2582